SLOTS
for the
CLUELESS

SLOTS
for the
CLUELESS

$\diamond$

A BEGINNER'S GUIDE TO PLAYING AND WINNING

John Patrick

LYLE STUART
Kensington Publishing Corp.
www.kensingtonbooks.com

LYLE STUART books are published by

Kensington Publishing Corp.
850 Third Avenue
New York, NY 10022

All Kensington titles, imprints, and distributed lines are available at special quantity discounts for bulk purchases for sales promotions, premiums, fund raising, educational, or institutional use. Special book excerpts or customized printings can also be created to fit specific needs. For details, write or phone the office of the Kensington special sales manager: Kensington Publishing Corp., 850 Third Avenue, New York, NY 10022, attn: Special Sales Department, phone 1-800-221-2647.

Lyle Stuart is a trademark of Kensington Publishing Corp.

First Kensington printing: November 2001

10 9 8 7 6 5 4 3 2 1

Printed in the United States of America

Library of Congress Control Number: 2001094199

ISBN 0-8184-0625-9

CONTENTS

PREFACE

Slots for the Clueless, that's the name of the book and it's not really for clueless people, but rather aimed at people who are clueless when it comes to gambling. In this case, we're going over the popular game of slots. The machines are buzzing throughout the casinos, in all parts of the world, by people who love to play these one-armed bandits.

So, play them. But play them intelligently and that means with a strong disciplined money-management approach.

There are methods and systems of betting on these pages, plus chapters that deal with handling your bankroll. Read these messages, but most of all, follow them to a "T." They will change the way you play slots!

PART I

Introduction

1

Introduction

Yeah, I know what you're gonna say, "How clueless do you have to be to play slots? All you gotta do is insert your coins in the right place and pull the handle." See, if you have to ask that question and make that statement, then you, too, are clueless in your approach to playing the slot machines.

This is my fourteenth book on gambling and if you have read any of them, you know doggone well where I'm heading with this one, and we're still on the first page. We're heading to what you really need to compete at any form of gambling. That "need" is called *money management* and it is required in any form of gambling. I don't care if you play bingo, toss pennies in the street, go to the race track, visit the casinos, bet on sports, or play poker with the boys or girls once a month. If you risk money on the outcome of an event, you are gambling. If you are gambling, you need money. If you've got money to gamble, then you need money management. You see, it's a vicious circle that encompasses most of us who enjoy putting a few dollars at risk in the hopes that we will kick off a payoff big enough to start dreaming of that "castle on the hill." Is it attainable? Anything is attainable if you have the right approach. But you must learn how to discipline yourself and how to use control. In other words, you gotta *learn how to win!*

Don't go pooh-poohing that last statement. Of course you gotta *learn* how to win. You gotta *learn* that there are ways to gamble sensibly.

There are thousands of people who enter the casinos every day and come away shaking their heads, stuffing their hands into empty pockets or cash-depleted pocketbooks, and wonder what the heck hit them. Nothing actually hit them. They just ran smack into a block called stupidity and ended up pouring their quarters and dollars into the coffers of a cold-hearted, noncaring string of one-armed bandits.

I am in the casinos four to five times a week. I bet on sports seven days a week. My outlets include blackjack, craps, roulette, poker, Pai Gow poker, baccarat and video poker in the casinos. I see other people at the tables, at the machines, and at the cashier windows. They are people like yourself and like me, looking to win a couple of dollars. Many of them play the slots and that is exactly what we will cover on these pages: How to play the slot machines! How to play *intelligently*.

I will lay out methods of play, called systems. But most of all I will give you money-management moves. Moves that will show you how to bet your money. Maybe you won't like all the methods, but you can bet the ranch you'll see some things that will improve your game plan. *Slots for the Clueless?* Yep, that's the name of the book and it's aimed at just such an audience.

2

The Big Four

It doesn't matter what you play, and it doesn't matter how much money you wager, there are certain guidelines that you need to be successful. I don't care if you're a green- and black-chip $100 craps player, or a 25-cent slots enthusiast, the list of items I am going to give you is imperative for your day of gambling.

I call them the Big Four and each and every one of them should be safely nestled in that area between your ears, as you enter the casino. Here are the Big Four and a short explanation of each:

1. Bankroll: This is the total amount of money you bring to battle. It don't mean diddley dang how much you bring, whatever the amount, that is your own personal bankroll. Every decision you make that day will be based on your separate bankroll. There will be a part devoted to this section of the Big Four shortly.

2. Knowledge of the Game: There will also be a part devoted to this section of the Big Four. Obviously, in playing the slots, there is less emphasis in this area, but you should know everything there is to know about the game you are risking your money on.

3. Money Management: This is the most important portion of your day and when you get to this part, you will see many

suggestions and variations of moves that you can and should make at the slots. Perhaps I can get across the total concept of what money management is—in one simple statement, "Money management is knowing what to bet after a win and what to bet after a loss." Sounds simple, and it is. But will you do it?

4. Discipline: Money management is the most important part of the Big Four, but discipline is the hardest to put into play. It is the thing that determines whether you will quit a winner on a given day and while we all say we have or want discipline, it seems to escape even the strongest of the strong.

My friend, I. M. Madork is a frequent visitor to Las Vegas and Atlantic City. He swears that he is a disciplined person and that he doesn't need help in that area. I asked him how disciplined he was and he explained, "I bring $300 to the casinos and hope to win $5,000. I play until I win that $5,000. I play only with the $300 I bring with me, plus only the $500 I withdraw from the ATM machines, and no more than $200 or $300 that the missus gives me. On any one day $1,000 is my disciplined max investment."

I asked him how often he won $5,000 with his starting bankroll of $300. His reply was, "Well, I've lost forty-three consecutive times, but there's always a first time for everything." I. M. Madork is, well, a *dork!* He has no discipline and probably never will. This lack of one part of the Big Four will always keep him in the losing bracket.

There you have the Big Four and in the next part we will go over bankroll. It starts your day.

3

The Reality of Gambling

You should by now know the importance of the Big Four. If you have all facets of what was laid out, you have a 50-50 chance of winning at gambling. I am the best player in the casino, the absolute perfect player.

1. I have a decent Bankroll to gamble with.
2. I know every single thing there is to know about the games I play.
3. I have a fabulous controlled and efficient set of money-management moves.
4. I have impeccable, unwavering discipline.

I have all four facets of the Big Four. My chances of winning, even with all of that, are 50-50. That's it! A 50-50 chance of winning. There are many other pros who also have full command of the Big Four. They too, have only a 50-50 chance of winning. That's the *reality* of gambling.

What do you think? Just because you have a fistful of dollars in your clammy hand, have the knowledge to be able to count to ninety-nine by threes, know the full impact of money management, and can spell dissaplin backwards, you have a head start at the casinos? Don't be silly! I. M. Madork has a better chance of driving into a pile of cow manure and coming out looking like Tom

Cruise than the average gambler has of going to the casinos and bringing them to their knees, day after day.

Gambling is rough and the house always holds the hammer. In roulette, there is a place on the table where you can bet on either red or black. Suppose you put your chip on red. They will pay you even money (equal to the amount you bet). There are eighteen red numbers, so you have eighteen ways to win. There are eighteen black numbers and two green ones. You have twenty ways to lose. That's 20-18 against you, and yet they only pay even money. You think that is not a big edge?

Try punching your buddy in the mouth eighteen times and he gets to punch you twenty times. Think that ain't a big edge in his favor? The house has a similar edge in every game on the floor— and that's the *reality* of gambling.

So, how do you overcome this edge? You don't, really, but by the proper use of your bankroll, by properly managing your money and by having impeccable discipline, you can forge winning days, if you have the brains and guts to quit with your profit. I'm gonna give you my most famous saying and I hope you memorize it. Don't worry, you don't have to memorize it right now, because I'll be giving it to you many times during the upcoming chapters, "Seventy percent of the people who enter a casino get ahead, during the course of their day. Yet 90 percent of that 70 percent give the money back!"

Think about that. We'll say 100 people walk into a casino. Seventy percent of them, 70 in all, will be ahead a decent amount during the course of their day. Yet 90 percent of that 70 percent (63 people) will give back those profits. That comes to 7 out of 100 people who will realistically walk out winning. I'll bet you, too, have fallen into this endless pit of stupidity. I know I have. *We all do!*

And that's the *reality* of gambling!

4

The Little Three

You've already got an idea of the main things (Big Four), that you must carry into the casino. It don't mean diddely dang what game you play, including slots, you must have the things I listed in the previous chapters.

But before we get into the bankroll part of your day, let's go over a couple of more things that can only help you, in your quest to bring home a profit. I call them the Little Three:

1. Theory: Is an opinion on how to play the slots. It could be at one or two or three machines, it could be at one single machine, or it could be a hit and run method at a tremendous number of different machines. Theory is also having an opinion on how much you will wager on each pull. Theory is never wrong. But you must develop your own theory and stick to it.

    I will be giving you my theory on how to play and how to bet and when to quit. It is *my* theory. You can either accept it or reject it.

2. Logic: You know what logic means. It is doing something that makes sense. You wouldn't dive out of an airplane without a parachute. That would be illogical. You wouldn't pick a fight with a 6'11", 325-pound wrestler. That would be illogical. You wouldn't go to a casino with your good hard-earned money,

without having all facets of the Big Four and Little Three. That would be *illogical*.

I will show you a logical (sensible) way to play and bet and a logical and sensible disciplined path to follow. You will see its logical results.

3. Trends: Ahhhh, this is the most important of all. In fact, I really should include it with the Big Four, because it is so important. *Trends* occur in gambling, more than you think. They also occur at the slot machines, whether you wanna believe it or not. *Do not* disregard the information that will be given to you on trends. In fact, a complete chapter will be devoted to this subject coming up. Do not pass it over.

There you have the Little Three and I hope you eventually see where that input can help make your trips to the slots more profitable. I will put a complete chapter on trends next but will be alluding to theory (mine) and logic (everybody's) as we go through the book. My friend Watt E. Cey is in a fog and doesn't grasp what I am saying right now. I hope you are not as dense as Watt E. Cey and know exactly what I am saying.

5

Trends

Yes, trends happen on slots and video poker machines, just like they happen on a roulette table, with that little plastic, weightless ball suddenly finding eight consecutive black areas to fall into. Or it will kick off nine straight odd numbers and you wonder how such a thing could happen. But it does.

Over at the craps table, twelve shooters in a row established a point and immediately sevened out, destroying every right bettor, who stubbornly ignored that trend and continued to put their money on the pass line. As the right bettors finally left the game, wiped out by that unbelievable cold streak, the don't bettors started increasing their bets to take advantage of that cold streak. It lasted for another fifteen minutes. Then a little old lady came up to the table, clutching the last three chips she had before oblivion and an early seat on the bus ride home. She could barely see over the table and had to stand on tiptoes to get the leverage to toss the dice across the felt.

Well, her toes got good exercise. She established four as her point and then threw seventeen consecutive place numbers before making her four. In the next forty-five minutes she made six points, besides an average of twelve place numbers during each game.

The red-hot streak continued until one of her tosses hit the hand of a jerk trying to get a late bet down. The die rolled a few inches and then stopped, completing a 7, which ended the hottest streak that casino had seen in six days, which of course followed the coldest streak on that table in two weeks.

Over in the blackjack section, a dealer ran off sixteen winning hands, crushing every would-be patron who dared sit at that particular table. Right next to that scorching hot-streaking dealer was a table where the dealer broke 21 on fourteen straight hands, prompting high fives from the seven lucky players who happened to be sitting at that table.

Yeah, trends happen both for and against us. It is our job, our responsibility, to quickly see these streaks and react. If they are going in our favor, we increase our bets. If they are going against us, we run. It's as simple as that, but many people are too stubborn (stupid) to see when things are going bad and hang in there, hoping (praying) that they will eventually change. How dumb!

Who can explain why trends occur? I certainly can't but have seen enough of them to know they are there. Take any two-headed coin and flip it one hundred times. Record each decision in order. It is 50-50 whether the decision will be heads or tails. But notice how often you'll see 6 heads in a row, 5 tails in a row, 8 tails, 6 heads. It goes in streaks or trends. Why? I dunno. But it does.

So the trick is taking advantage of those trends and that will be done in the part on money management. So just hold your britches.

6

Computers in Slots

Don't scoff at that statement. I just finished showing you how a set of dice in craps, a weightless, plastic ball in roulette and paper cards in blackjack can run in streaks, why not a machine full of bolts and nuts and a "computer"?

Oops, did I say computer? How nasty of me. How terrible to suggest that the casinos would even dare to dream of clouding up a slot machine with one of those new-fangled contraptions that can determine patterns, streaks, or trends, or winnings or losings. But the plain fact of the matter is that computers have become a big part of the gambling world and it is not uncommon to find them lodged in the caverns of the popular slot machines and video poker machines.

Many years ago, when I first got involved in gambling, there were these slot machines out in Las Vegas whereby if you inserted your nickel (yeah, I said nickel) into the slot, the wheels would start spinning and run until they would run out of steam. You got a random result. You had a fair chance of getting three 7s, or three oranges or three plums or a couple of cherries.

In other words—you had a fair shot of winning a couple of jack-pots. Of course the high rollers played the quarter machines and the veddy, veddy rich visitors from Hollywood sat in front of the dollar machines. I could only dream of having enough money to play dollar slots (of which there were very few in those days).

Anyhow, the years passed and the geniuses of the world came up with inventions that were mind boggling:

1. You could turn on a thing called a radio and hear music.
2. You could sit and watch a screen with moving figures called TV.
3. You could put a thing up to your ear and talk personally to your bookie, called a telephone.
4. You could do anything in the world, *anything*, except drink coffee, with a thing called a computer.

A lot of these things are foreign to me. (I'm still trying to figure out how water comes out of a faucet.)

Zero in on number 4 and the addition of these computers to our lives. The casino community, no dummies, mind you, figured out that it was better to allow the computers to become part of slot machines, in order to assure that a glitch doesn't allow the machines to run amuck and kick off so many jackpots that the casinos could get whacked. Hence the industry use of a computer chip to control the percentage of returns from a slot machine. This way, the unwary slot player can still win his jackpot, but no way will the casinos allow for a runaway bonanza on any machine. There will be cold streaks, usually following a big hit, but we'll touch on that in the next chapter. Computers in slots? Welcome to the real world!

7

Trends in Slots

Casinos Don't Cheat! Let's make that clear right now. They don't have to cheat to win money. There are so many dumb players who enter the casinos every day, why should they even have to worry about cheating? And they don't!

So the machines are not "fixed," in that you have no chance of winning. Sure, you'll hear people claim:

1. Hey, these machines are fixed.
2. The house rigs the machines.
3. You can't win at this casino.
4. All casinos cheat.

The answer is *no* to all of the above. You lose because you probably lack the all-important needs of money management and discipline.

Do the computers hinder your chances of hitting it big at a machine? The answer to that question is a resounding yes. That's because the computers are there to protect the casinos' interests; to make sure that the payoffs don't exceed the amount of return that is required by law.

In Atlantic City, the machines must return at least 87 percent. In Vegas returns are more liberal, because they use slots as "loss leaders" (i.e., to lure customers into the casino).

Some slots in Vegas will kick off 92-93-94-95 percent returns. The casinos can live quite happily with heavy action and allow better returns. So forget the cheating nonsense and think about trends. Trends definitely occur in gambling and I already went over this fact.

There are two kinds of trends in gambling. They are distinguished by the terms: hot streaks and cold streaks. My friend Izzy Kold is a jerk. He doesn't realize that when he is playing a slot machine and has lost fifteen straight pulls, that the machine is in a cold streak. His illogical thought is that his "luck" will change. He's crazy. You should never get stuck at a machine in a cold streak, in a cold trend.

Don't worry, in the next part you'll see "loss limits" and "naked pulls," which will protect you from getting stuck in these losing trends, so just be patient.

In the same vein, my friend Red Hott will be playing at a machine that is red hot. On twenty-three consecutive pulls, he has gotten a return. But Red doesn't take advantage of that trend. He keeps inserting 1 coin at a time into that slot. I ask him, "Hey Red, that machine is in a hot trend, why not increase your bet?" The answer is, "Nah, it's due to cool off." Later on I see him at a frigid machine, that has not kicked off even 1 coin in fourteen straight decisions. He is betting max coins. I ask him: "Hey Red, that machine is frigid, why are you playing it?" His answer is, "Hey, I'm due to win. It's due to change!"

He's wrong all the way around. You are *never* due to win. You do *not* bet more when losing and less when winning. You have to learn how to recognize and then handle trends, because they do occur. I'll show you later on, or have I said that before?

8

Smart Slot Play

The name of this book is *Slots for the Clueless.* So what is the remedy for a clueless person? Answer: A solution.

This book and the chapters on your approach to gambling in general and slots in particular, will show you two things:

1. How to cut losses at the slots.

2. How to intelligently take profits from slots play home with you.

This first section was designed to give you a first-hand look at what is needed for you to compete intelligently in the casinos.

Question: Should you play the slots?

Answer: My opinion is no. There are better games to play than the slots. But it is not my right to condemn anyone for playing the game of their choice. My mother plays the slots and I have been taking her to A.C. for the past twenty years, two to three times a week. Of course she plays other games like video poker, Pai Gow poker, roulette and Let It Ride, but 20 percent of her action is on slots. You wanna play slots, go ahead. I will show you *how* to intelligently play them.

Question: Is playing slot machines the worst game in the house?

Answer: No! (You thought I was gonna say yes.) But no, it is not the worst, in comparison to people who play other games, with their limited amount of knowledge of that other particular game.

Keep this in mind. There is a set return for the slot machines, which I already covered. For example, I'll use the 87 percent return for A.C. casinos. The slot player knows he will get that percentage—but obviously spread over millions of decisions.

A blackjack player is competing at a game with only a so-called 2 or 3 percent house vig (vigorish or "house edge" or advantage). But that is *only* if that person is a perfect basic-strategy player. If they don't know basic strategy, the vig against them could be 20 percent, 30 percent, or even 40 percent. So slots is not the worst game, from a standpoint of built-in house edge. Caribbean Stud gets that honor, plus a little game with a big wheel, called the "Big Wheel." Those two games should be avoided. So what is smart slot play? Glad you asked, because it is the title of this chapter. But it takes a lot of various inputs.

Starting with the next section, I will show you how to tie your entire "slot playing days" into a neat little package. It will be hard for you to do this, because it is structured and contains money management and discipline requirements.

The results of this chore? You will no longer be clueless and will be a smart player. Will you win every day? Of course not, but on the days that the machines are in a down trend—your losses will be reduced—dramatically!

PART II

Bankroll

9

Loss Limits

Go back and read the last paragraph of the preceding chapter.
That sets the stage for this all-important lesson in gambling and
keys one of my most famous sayings, "It ain't how much you win in
gambling that is important. It is how little you lose that matters."
This is one of the most important chapters in the book and it kicks
off our first look at the Big Four: Bankroll! What is bankroll? It is
how much money you bring to the casino to gamble with.

What are loss limits? Pretty easy to figure that out. It is the
amount of money you will lose on a particular day—and quit!
Hence the term "loss limits"! We've all gone to a casino and lost
money, because nobody wins all the time. That's impossible. Even
pros lose, not because they're dumb or forget how to play on a
certain day, but because these trends I talked about previously,
were against them. On those days and during those sessions, the
key is cutting those losses to the bone. What a lousy feeling it is to
leave the casino, down $100 or $300 or $500 or even $1,000. It is
a sinking, empty feeling of frustration. The higher the loss, the
more devastated we are. I set loss limits that protect my overall
bankroll on those days when I can't find a hot table or machine.
My loss limits are more important than my win goals.

What is my loss limit for machine play? I'll let you figure it out.
Give me a number between 59 and 61. I'll give you the answer in
a minute, but here is an important tip: *never* play down to your

final amount of coins. Never go to a machine, for example with $20, and lose that whole amount. Set a loss limit.

Do you think if you have played $14 or $16 or $18 at that machine and got zilch, that the last handful of coins are gonna recoup all those losses? Don't be silly. That is a cold machine and you gotta rely on your loss limit to protect you. If you haven't figured it out by now, the loss limit should not be a quarter or a dollar more than 60 percent of your bankroll.

Congrats to those who figured it out. Now you can set 30 percent, 40 percent, or 50 percent, whatever you feel comfortable with. But the max is a solid 60 percent.

Coming up in a couple of chapters is another loss limit called "naked pulls," so we'll go back to this subject again. For now—stick to a 60 percent loss limit per machine (session), and no cheating! Remember—60 percent!

10

Win Goals

No, you can't march in to a casino and say:

1. "I wanna win as much as I can."
2. "I just wanna triple my bankroll."
3. "I'll play until I either lose what I brought or take home what I have, when it's time to leave."

There is nothing intelligently structured in any of those statements. There is no attempt to discipline yourself, to accept an intelligent profit. Remember, you are playing a game that has the odds stacked against you, even if you are a perfect player. I am a perfect player. All pros are perfect players. We have all facets of the Big Four. We realize the danger of gambling and are willing (in fact ecstatic), to grab a 10 percent or glory be, a 20 percent return on our investment. Maybe that don't seem like a lot to you, but figure it out from a standpoint of everyday reality.

You have $1,000 that you stick in the bank for a year and you brag to me what a financial genius you are because you found a place that is giving you 6 percent interest. You're gonna make $60 for the year on that investment.

Then you take another $1,000 to the casino and play games, whereby you have no clue about money management or discipline and the house holds the vigorish edge over you. You get ahead $60 after two hours. Do you quit? No way, because it ain't enough to make it worth your while. Can you imagine a person with thinking like that? He is happy with $60 for a year but not happy with a $60 return in one day. Go figure!

A pro is satisfied with small percentage returns. A novice wants to break the bank. You must set a win goal and while 10 percent or 20 percent will never be accepted by the daily visitor, who brings $200 or $300 or $400 to battle, at least work out a percentage that you will be content with.

Let's put it at 50 percent for those people that have limited bankrolls. Admittedly that is a trifle high, so I'll list a scale that will be a little aggressive, but you can make slight revisions, if you see fit.

Bankroll	Win Goal
$100	60%
$200	50%
$300	40%
$400	30%
$500 or higher	25%

This does not mean you will quit when your goal is reached, but it is a goal to shoot for. Note that the higher amount you bring, the lower win goal you aim for. Later on in the money management and discipline section, I will elaborate on a method called "guarantee and excess."

We will go deeper, but for now, here is an example: You get ahead $120 with a $300 starting bankroll.

1. Take that starting $300 bankroll and put it in your pocket.
2. Take the $120 you are ahead (your win goal), and break it in half.
3. Fifty percent ($60) is put in your pocket. It is called your "guarantee." You are guaranteed to bring home a profit of at least $60.

4. The other 50 percent ($60) is kept in play. It is called your "excess." You continue playing with that excess in hopes of increasing profits.

I will go over variations of handling that excess later on, but do you now see the power of setting a win goal—and knowing how to handle it?

Win goals! Set them!

11

The Importance of Bankroll

You know, I don't think I can emphasize enough, the power of a good solid bankroll. Better still, I can't emphasize enough the drawback of not having enough money. Playing with a short bankroll will cause you to play scared, and scared playing makes you play stupid. Playing stupid in a casino is a one-way trip to getting whacked.

So, it is simply imperative that you realize the importance of being able to play comfortably. *That* is the reason that this message is repeated in this section. I see so many people trying to stretch a bankroll of $40 or $50 into a day's gambling, and you know doggone well that they will go home broke. The reason they bring only a small amount to gamble with is—none of my business. It could be lack of funds, or a reluctance to bring a lot of money for fear that they will gamble more, if they bring more.

They are not wrong about having those drawbacks of small funds or lack of discipline. If you fall into one of those categories, bear with me, as these situations will be addressed in later chapters and sections.

In a perfect world, you would be able to bring $1,000 to the slot section, play max coins, win a jackpot on every visit you make, and go home each night with your pockets filled with cash. But alas and alack, this is not a perfect world. Most people don't have the means to bring a big bankroll to the casinos, are usually forced to play single coins, have never tasted the fruits of having a jackpot explode on their machine, and simply don't have the discipline to know when to quit.

If any of the situations mentioned in this chapter ring close to home, don't get discouraged. You are not among the minority when it comes to going to the casinos "unprepared." Sorry I gotta use that harsh a word, but if the shoe fits, wear it. By the time you finish this book, and if you follow all the rules, not just the ones you wanna follow, you will see a positive reversal from any losing days you usually have had to endure.

12

Sessions

Handling your bankroll is a prime necessity in the casinos. It's important that you protect it, because when it is gone, you're dead in the water. You'll have nothing to compete with. Since trends are so dominant at the machines, you don't wanna take your entire bankroll to that first machine. One long cold spell and you've gone too deep into your operating capital.

Divide your bankroll into equal machines, called "sessions." This way you have a like amount of money to invest into a number of machines. The amount of machines you decide to play at, should be decided before you hit the floor. This way an equal amount of your bankroll can be allotted to each machine. Here are suggestions for amounts to take to a machine:

Bankroll	# of Sessions	Per Session Amount
$100	10	$10
$200	10	$20
$200	20	$10
$200	5	$40
$300	10	$30
$300	20	$15
$300	15	$20
$300	30	$10

You get the idea. You either go to a lot of machines with smaller session amounts or to a few machines with higher amounts. The choice is yours. With $200 my opinion would be ten sessions. With $300 my opinion would be ten sessions for $30 each.

Don't shrug off the breaking of your initial bankroll down into sessions. Some people like to plop in front of a certain machine at the beginning of their day and stay there for hours, playing their entire bankroll at that machine.

Their contention is that soon a hot streak will occur. Sorry, I can't buy that idea. That computer chip will rear its ugly decisions as soon as a couple of decent payoffs show. I don't wanna be ground out by several long losing streaks.

Incidentally, every session has its own win goal and loss limit and on the subject of the latter, I told you there would be another message applied to the loss-limit percentage.

It is called "naked pulls"! How convenient. Look at the title of the next chapter.

13

Naked Pulls

You're already aware of how much I lean toward holding down losses. You don't realize it yet, but that is what gambling is all about. The wins will come. The trick is keeping your losses to such a minimum that when you do hit the hot streak, you don't have a lot of losses to recoup.

Well, along with the chapter on loss limit, we have another method of getting you away from a machine that is going bad. The method is called "naked pulls" and you don't need to be a rocket scientist to figure out what it means. "Naked" means "nothing" and "pulls" stands for "plays." If you are getting nothing over a series of plays, then that machine is cold.

Deciding on how long it takes to determine if a machine is cold needs very little figuring. Think of a number between seven and fourteen. That number will be your naked pulls. You gotta give the machine at least seven pulls, but when you reach the teens, it's fairly obvious you've encountered an iceberg.

Let's suppose you pick ten as your naked pulls. The instant you reach ten pulls that kickoff zilch, you wrap up that session. My friend Juan Moore will say just one more pull and I'll leave. But that is unacceptable. One more leads to another, and another, and before you know it, you find yourself chasing fool's gold.

The gold is the coins you keep pouring in. You already know who the fool is.

With the use of two separate protections of your session money, it is now safe to say that you can't be knocked out at a single machine. Look at the theories:

1. Loss Limits: With a strict loss limit of 60 percent of the amount of the session money, you have a built-in protection against losing everything at one machine. Another power of loss limits is if the naked-pull number you set doesn't get reached. Let's say ten is your naked pulls! You could lose seven straight, win one, lose six straight, win one, lose eight straight, win one. See what's happening? You ain't hitting your naked pulls but you're being ground out. The loss limit protects you in these instances.

2. Naked Pulls: I know it's tough to keep moving to different machines, but when cold trends hit these machines, it ain't uncommon for twelve to fourteen straight zippo's to occur. I've given you two protections.

I hope you see the power of cutting losses. I know it is a structured approach to gambling, something you never had before— but it sure does work.

14

Reality II

Yeah, I know, you already got a dose of reality in a prior chapter. But get to live with these references to this subject because it ain't the last one you'll get. Gambling is a rough, addictive, fascinating, and humbling experience to anyone who ventures onto the casino floor. Senior citizens, with limited resources and engaging in slots play because they won't play the table games, are subjected to the biggest disappointments because of their persistence in playing only the slots.

Again, I am not condemning their choice of game, only emphasizing the fact that even the slots players have to be subjected to the same discipline rules as table players. Why did you purchase this book? My humble opinion is that you wanted to see if there was a certain secret or magic formula for playing the slots.

Well, to people who spend their lives gambling, like me, there is no big secret or formula. It is the realization that gambling is a rough road, but it is possible to bang out a nice winning day, if and I repeat *if*—you adopt a controlled way of playing. So far, I've given you a look at the slot players themselves, and the things they need to compete intelligently.

This particular section is aimed at showing you how to handle the bankroll you have to work with. Once you grasp the things I am giving you, getting you ready for actual play, we'll show you how to bet the money you bring. That will be covered in the next part and as important as those moves are, the ones covered here are just as important.

A car needs many components to operate successfully. The motor alone will not get you anywhere. A successful business needs the input of many people with different skills, all contributing something to make that business operate successfully. Gambling is no different. All of the things touched on so far are pieces of a puzzle that will get you into a position to play intelligently.

Nah, you won't like the controls and restrictions I put on your play. You'll say you just wanna play for fun and entertainment. Horse feathers! You wanna win money just as much as I do.

The doctor's medicine doesn't taste good but you realize it is in your best interests. The information I give to you sounds too restrictive but trust me, it's good for you. Will it make you win all the time? Heck no, but it'll keep you in this very, very tough quest for success at a tough game.

And that my friends, is the *reality* of gambling!

15

Scared Money

It's important that we look at this area of bankroll because it affects so many of us. It is the size or amount of one's bankroll, that restricts one's play. Because of his economic situation, he may be hindered by the lack of a sizable bankroll. In other words, he doesn't have a lot of money to bring to battle.

My friend, Shorty Shortkash, is a little short of cash. He has about $100 to take to the machines, so obviously he is limited in the amount of his bets and the amount of sessions he can play at.

Shorty Shortkash likes to play the 50¢ and $1 machines, but in his financial situation, this is strictly taboo. He barely has enough cash to break it into ten machines at a sawbuck per session at the quarter machines. But his lack of sufficient funds will cause him to play *scared*.

My friend Lotta Kash has no problem bringing a couple of thousand dollars to the casinos. With her bankroll she can play at the dollar machines and set aside decent amounts of session money.

Even though she has the money to withstand losing streaks, she definitely should not stray from the rules laid out about loss limits. But her available cash does put her in a better position than that of Shorty Shortkash. That can be a big plus for her, because she definitely need not worry about having the money to play at many sessions, looking for a hot machine.

If you are in a position like Shorty, being hampered by a lack of funds, either cut back on your win goals or wait until you are properly bankrolled, before coming to the casinos. It is not a crime to be in a monetary shortfall. We all go through those periods. It is a crime to be in such a position and play like a jerk, thinking you may hit the jackpot and ease your money woes. That's terrible thinking.

If you are short of cash, wait until you accumulate a proper bankroll. If you play short, you'll play scared. If you play scared, you'll play stupid. If you play stupid, you'll lose. It's as simple as that.

16

Wrapping Up Bankroll

Well, I guess we've given you enough of an insight into the importance of the first part of the Big Four, bankroll, to get you started. Don't lose sight of the fact that whatever the size of the bankroll you have to operate with is very, very important in how you lay out your session amounts.

Of course you'd like to have a healthy two or three thousand barrels of cash with which to attack those machines. Who wouldn't?

But the reality of it is that most people have to operate with limited funds. You ain't the only person in the casino playing on a so-called shoestring. That don't give you the right to play like a jerk. It is such a great feeling to leave that casino with a profit. Not many people get that thrill because they refuse to quit when they have a nice little profit burning a hole in their pocket. They offer themselves these outs:

1. "Hey, so what that I'm up a lousy $50. I didn't come here to win a paltry fifty bucks." (This boob started with $100 and is up 50 percent of what he began with.)

2. "I won't be here for another month or so. So what if I give back this profit. I had a day in the casinos."

3. "I'd be embarrassed to tell my friends I only won $40 and quit. They'd call me a cheapskate. I'm gonna go back and take a real shot." (So he loses back everything.)

How many times have you heard someone (maybe yourself) utter those ridiculous statements? Of course on the way home, they see the error of their thoughts but by then it's too late.

The suggestions I laid out for you are not as bad as getting a stick in the eye. They are proven guidelines that will change your gambling days. They are geared to:

1. Kick off intelligent returns.
2. Cut losses to the bone.

I have a web site. It is www.johnpatrick.com. Go there sometime (if you have a computer) and read the comments of people who have adopted my conservative style of gambling. They rave about getting small but consistent returns. They even agree that bringing home small profits, beats going home broke.

OK, we've finished bankroll and next we get to the second part of the Big Four (Knowledge of the Game). Before moving on, do me a favor (and yourself). Go back and read the chapters on win goals and loss limits.

Once those theories are locked into your thinking, you're starting to become a *real* player.

PART III

Knowledge of the Game

17

Knowledge of the Game

In every one of my fourteen books, I used the same format, starting with the first one, back in 1984, which was *Blackjack*. That format called for a section on introducing the game I was discussing, then a section dedicated to each facet of the Big Four. The final part is always dedicated to Odds and Ends, you know, the things that pertain to a person going to the casinos.

Why should I change the format? It was the proper way to approach gambling back in the mid-eighties and it is the same today.

The Big Four are needed to give you a shot at gambling and each part is necessary. But with slot machines, we have a problem. How much "knowledge" do you need to play the slots? You just insert your coins, pull the handle and watch (pray), to see what happens. You are surely not interested in how they build the machines and I doubt if the casinos will give us the keys to slots, so we can study its main parts.

So, maybe knowledge ain't so important in the category of slot machines. But before you close your mind to the messages in this section, get to understand what I said before. All parts of the Big Four are necessary.

Just for emphasis, I'm gonna take three messages and give you a reminder of their importance. If you wanna call it knowledge—good. If you wanna say it ain't knowledge—you're wrong!

I'm writing this book and I say these messages are important. You'll read them.

1. *Computer Chip:* I've already told you that the casinos don't cheat and they don't. But keep in mind that we are fighting a chip—that makes sure the casino does not get stuck with a machine that is tilted too much in our favor.

2. *Trends:* Yeah, machines run hot and cold. Usually after a giant hit, that old trend runs completely in the opposite direction. It is important that you know about and follow the naked pulls and loss limits, that are there to protect you.

3. *Due Slots:* You are *never* due to win at the slots or for that matter any part of gambling. God does not "allow" you to win, just because you've lost between seven and nine pulls in a row. If you're at a cold machine, then you're at a cold machine. Don't be a dork and keep pouring coins into that machine, thinking it's gonna even out over the next ten to twenty pulls. Leave that machine as soon as your first loss limit kicks in.

There are a couple more chapters on knowledge that might benefit you. When was the last time knowledge didn't benefit everyone?

Read the chapters!

18

Who Plays the Slots?

You're reading a book entitled *Slots for the Clueless*, and you have to wonder about that? Actually, a lot of players are engaged in some sort of machine play, whether it be slots or video poker machines.

Many years ago, when I first ventured into the world of Las Vegas, where gambling was trying to get a foothold on the emotions of a cautious country, the slots were the biggest draw.

All the movies in the 1940s and 1950s always portrayed the gad guy as a gambler. Bogard, Cagney, Raft, even Gable in *Gone With the Wind*, were cast as gamblers, and they all wore black.

Gambling was a dark side of our culture and crap games were always shown being played in back alleys. Bookies met you in dark rooms or in parked cars. Going to Vegas meant you had to go to confession when you returned.

I was in Vegas back in the late fifties and early sixties when there were only a handful of casinos. Blackjack was popular as a table game, craps so-so, roulette tables were empty, and baccarat was played for cash (not chips), and only the veddy, veddy rich pulled up a chair in those plush quarters.

Visitors oohed and ahhed at the table games and then rushed to pour their nickels into the slots. It was easy, nobody noticed you, or questioned your lack of knowledge of gambling and most of all, you had a decent chance of converting your roll of nickels into a nice payoff. Computer chips were not yet invented, and the casinos were so glad to get your business that they were willing to suffer some losses at machines operating strictly on random decisions.

Well, things ain't changed much today; people still rush to the slots, hoping to go tone deaf when their machine bangs out three jackpot symbols. The casinos let the bells ring forever when a jackpot (rarely) shows, hoping to attract all patrons to partake in slots playing.

As I said before, slots ain't the best game in the house, because it eats your coins like a desert devours a few drops of water.

But who does play the slots? If I were to go back in time and list the types of people I have seen inserting coins into a machine, the list would look something like this:

1. Men
2. Women
3. Young people
4. Old people
5. Senior citizens
6. Single people
7. Married couples
8. Tall people
9. Short people
10. Fat people
11. Skinny people
12. Well-dressed people
13. Slobs
14. Rich people
15. Poor people
16. Liberals

17. Conservatives

18. Drunks

19. Sober people

20. Everybody

Yep, everybody has at one time or another, invested a coin or two into these one-armed bandits.

Today, there are a thousand different versions of slots: three reels, five reels, ten reels, 25¢, $1, $5, and even $25 slots.

And who plays these slots? Everybody! It ain't for me to judge. My purpose is to show you *how* to play!!!

19

Quarter or Dollar Slots?

That is not a question you have the right to ask. Your *bankroll* tells you what type of machine you can go to. Your bankroll determines all of your money decisions. If you have an amount of money in the $100 to $300 range, you need only work out the numbers to see why going to the big machines is suicide.

Let's suppose $300 is your total bankroll and you agree with my theory of breaking that cash into equal sessions. Let us also assume that you will abide by the loss limit restrictions that I put on each session (60 percent).

You walk into the slot section with $300 and decide to break that money into ten sessions of $30 each. That's an intelligent distribution of funds. You have ten different machines and a decent amount of money ($30) to take a decent shot.

Based on the 60 percent loss limit, $18 is the most you can lose at each of those sessions. You have enough money to sustain you comfortably at a quarter machine. But now let's say you take that same amount of money ($300), and same game plan to the dollar machines. You plan on starting with 2 coins per play and increase your wagers, as the machine gets hot.

You go to the first machine and insert $2, playing the "up the steps" method that I will explain in the next section. Anyhow, five pulls later, which is not uncommon with the slots, you are out $10 because nothing has shown to kick off a return.

You are out $10 of the $30 you allocated to this first machine. Since 60 percent of $30 (your loss limit) gives you only $18 to risk per machine, you are already over 50 percent into your playable cash.

And you haven't stayed at that machine long enough to even cast a shadow. Think about it. At a quarter machine, using 2 coins to start, $30 is an excellent cushion for a losing streak. That's because you are risking quarters. But that same $30, at a dollar machine, risking $2 per play, will bury you often, unless you get off to a quick start.

Adjusting your play to start with the insertion of 3 coins per play, will still leave you comfortable at a quarter machine, even in the face of a losing streak. But three-unit play, at a dollar machine, with a $30 stake, is walking the high wire between buildings on Park Avenue in New York, without a net!

Your bankroll determines the value of the machine you go to. With a stake of $300, your best (and your most intelligent) shot is at the quarter machines.

You wanna bet more? Bring more! Unless you are blessed with at least $1,000 working capital, which allows you to play comfortably at several machines, your action should be geared to the quarter machines.

Again—if you wanna win more, bring more, or have I said that before?

20

Nickel Machines

Since we're taking a very basic look at playing the slots, I think it is only natural that a chapter is pointed to the nickel slots. I've already told you that the casinos, many years ago, were jammed with the nickel slots. If you found a dollar machine in those days, some business giant or movie star was playing it. The rest of us just stood in awe and watched that "high roller" do what we longed to do: Bet the big bucks!

Of course money had a different value then. There was value in money and a buck got you something in return.

1. It cost a quarter to go to a movie.

2. Gasoline was 19 cents a gallon.

3. Candy bars were a nickel.

4. You could ride the bus for a nickel.

5. A loaf of bread was 11 cents.

6. You could buy a new car for $1,500 (or less).

7. You got comped a room, meal, and show tickets for playing the nickel slots.

8. A cup of coffee was a nickel.

9. Athletes were paid what they were worth (very little).

10. Politicians were overpaid. (What's new there?)

The point I'm trying to make is that there were machines available that gave people with short bankrolls, a decent shot. Today there are still many 5-cent slots on all the casino floors. Recently, in a certain Atlantic City casino, which shall remain nameless, they just put in over two hundred more nickel machines.

The senior citizens are flocking to play these mechanical robbers. Why do they rush to play these types of machines? Because they require a lower amount of money to compete. Hey, you can play max coins for just a quarter. Of course the relative profit is also low, but at least these people have a machine that fits their bankroll.

Should you play the 5-cent machines? Let me put it this way. I take my mother, 94 years old and counting, to the casinos twice and sometimes three times a week. This has been going on for twenty years and she loves the action. She plays slots, video poker, roulette, Pai Gow poker and Let It Ride. (I told you this already but am repeating it for effect.) I won't let her play the 5-cent slots. It is important that I qualify that statement because it has two definitive answers:

1. It is my humble opinion that the payoffs on the 5-cent slots are not in line for what payoffs *should be!* The people who play 5-cent slots are mostly seniors and people with small bankrolls. Good grief! Give these people a break. Raise the payoff percentage to a decent 90 percent to 95 percent so that these people have a shot. It ain't gonna break these money-grabbing casinos to give certain people a better shot. And seniors and people in poor economic situations deserve a break. That is why I won't let my mother play 5-cent slots. She is not getting a break.

2. I think people with short bankrolls should play the 5-cent slots. They have less chance of losing a lot of money on these value machines.

Sorry I talked out of both sides of my mouth on this subject. But in a nutshell, I'll repeat it:

1. Five-cent slots don't give a decent (better) chance for their players.
2. You *gotta* play them, if your economic situation dictates it.

Think about the messages I gave you in this chapter!

21

Machines and Vigorish

Man, how I hate to write this chapter, but I got to. It has to do with knowledge of the machines and has zippo to do with helping you win. But if I don't fill you in, even if the info is boring, then I am doing you a disservice. So, here goes!

The house has an edge on every game and every machine on the floor. That's the way it is and that's the way it should be. If you can't handle this fact, then you have no right in the casino.

They pay the rent (from *our* losings), the electric bill, the salaries, and everything else that has to do with running the casino. We can play if we like, or just walk around with our hands in our pockets, wishing we owned the joint. If we do decide to risk our money, then we do it with the knowledge that the house now has the edge. But that does not mean we can't get ahead a couple of dollars—and quit with our profits.

You're not chained to that machine and the casinos don't say you have to continue playing until you're broke. They just know that most folks will give that money back. *Repeat!* "Seventy percent of the people who enter a casino get ahead, yet 90 percent of that 70 percent give it back!" Or have I said that before?

I've already told you that the slots return anywhere from 87 percent to 94 percent of every dollar bet. That's the law. A.C. is 87 percent but, of course, they can make the machines as loose as they want. Las Vegas, as is my understanding, can make the machines kick off as high a percentage as they want—and they do. They use it to get people to their houses. I am not sure what the minimum return is but the casinos all know this, because there are laws to protect the players, inasmuch as a certain percentage *has* to be repaid. I have no idea who watches the store (casino percentage returns) on cruise lines, riverboats or Indian casinos. I guess you have to go to the top to get your answer. But stop crying about the house having the hammer every time you lose at the machines. The fact of the matter is that you probably don't quit when you get ahead because you wanna win more with your starting bankroll than is intelligently possible. If you can't live with smart, small, consistent returns, then get a new outlet for your gambling days.

It is my humble opinion, that getting a set of 87 percent on the slots and video-poker machines, beats going to a blackjack table, where a bad unknowledgeable player, who doesn't know the difference between a split and surrender, is fighting a much higher vig. He or she is in worse shape than the slot player.

22

The Reality of Slots

Once again, turn back the hands of time and focus your thoughts on what the original slots were like. Very simple and uncomplicated. There were three reels to a machine and each reel contained twenty symbols (cherries, plums, oranges, lemons, etc.). There was a designated jackpot if three of the same symbol showed, and lesser returns for three oranges, for example, that would drop 14 coins into the tray, for each coin wagered.

Let's say three watermelons was the biggie. If they showed on each of the three reels, you got the payoff, maybe 200 coins, and your joy would have no bounds. All you had to do was insert your coin or multiple coins, pull the handle and wait for the reels to "run out of gas." A six-year-old child could repair these machines in the unlikely event that they misfired.

Let's say we opened that machine to observe the workings. Sure enough, there were three reels and the aforementioned twenty symbols on each reel. The more astute among us would go a step further. "I wonder what the chances of three watermelons showing up would be!" He would calculate the number of possible combinations on a three-wheel machine, with twenty possible stops.

Multiply the twenty symbols on reel number 1 by the twenty on reel number 2 and you have $20 \times 20 = 400$. Then multiply that four hundred by the twenty symbols on reel number 3 and you have $20 \times 400 = 8,000$. If there was only one watermelon symbol on each reel, you would have one chance in 8,000 of getting the jackpot. Our math wizard would be in shock.

But then that figure could be reduced by computing the number of watermelon symbols on each reel. You see, there are 8,000 combinations to work with and if there were only one symbol per reel, that is where the "chances of your winning" would come from. If the "house" wished to "make the machine looser," they did not have a computer to adjust, or have to fiddle with the mechanics. All they had to do was add a symbol to one of the reels and the chances of that combination showing all of a sudden got better. Word would spread about the "looseness" of certain casinos and folks would rush there. Yet all that was done was the simple matter of planting another watermelon in the garden. Let's say there were five watermelons on the first reel, four on the second reel, and three on the third. Simply multiply $5 \times 4 = 20$, then multiply 20×3 (third reel total), and your chances of getting that jackpot is 60 chances in 8,000 combinations.

For thinking purposes only, let us fast forward to today's machines, where there are maybe thirty or forty symbols to a reel, plus and I repeat *plus* the frustrating *blank*, which does no player any good, except that machines (glory be) give your money back if three blanks show!

If you were shocked to find that there are 8,000 possible combinations on a twenty-symbol three-reel machine, let me give you an arithmetic result. In today's world, discounting a thirty-symbol reel, let us go to a twenty-symbol plus twenty-blank three-reel machine and see what the possible number of combinations would be, based on forty stops on each reel.

Let's see, forty (first reel) times forty (second reel) equals $40 \times 40 = 1,600$. Adding in the third reel, we get $1,600 \times 40 = 64,000$ possible combinations. That is based on only one symbol per reel per pull, remember. But there are now 64,000 combos.

Today you can find five-reel machines (super jackpots), so let's for smiles, carry out the possible number of combinations that could occur on one of these babies: 64,000 (first 3 reels) × 40 (fourth reel), 64,000 × 40 = 2,560,000. Adding the fifth reel, we get 2,560,000 × 40 = One hundred and two million, four hundred thousand (102,400,000) combos.

Of course I'm being facetious to make a point, but I'm trying to get you to see the fight we're up against and how the more combos (reels), the more less of a chance we have (Yes, I said more less of a chance).

Here's your homework for the day. Use a five-reel twenty-stop machine, where ten stops are symbols and ten are blanks. What are the total number of possible combinations that could occur? Answer at end of next chapter.

I hate this chapter—but I want you to be an "aware player" the next time you venture up to a slot machine. Don't forget: I am only giving you total number of possible combos. The number of symbols (7s, triple bars, double bars, etc.) per reel is up to the casinos.

You gotta ask them to open the machine so you can count the number of symbols per reel, so as to figure your chances. Good luck landing, as they unceremoniously boot your behind out into the street!

23

Should I Play Slots?

What a question, and one I don't have a right to answer. First of all you should determine why you gamble in the first place. Everyone has a reason as to why they put money at risk for a chance to satisfy a *need* in their life. That *need* could be:

1. Win money.
2. Play for entertainment.
3. An outlet.
4. To be part of the ambiance of the casino gambling scene.
5. For fun.
6. Walking on the edge.

All of the above will or could be attributed to everyone who enters the doors of the casinos, wherever they may be. Personally, I am affected by the lure of number 1 and number 6. I gamble for money and I admit it. I love the thrill of walking on the edge, the ability to win at a set of games that are very difficult to dominate.

Maybe you gamble for fun, or just to get out of the house. A senior citizen gets bored staring at four walls and finds the lively environment of the casino life very stimulating. Gambling has absolutely exploded in this country and will only get bigger. More people are attracted to it than ever before.

There are those who play strictly craps, blackjack, or roulette. Others concentrate strictly on poker or the race tracks. The sports bettor is a different breed than all the others. They compete daily and it seems every single contest is decided in the last inning, last pitch, last play, or at the buzzer. And yet the hooked sports bettor returns the next day to take another shot. Maybe your game is video poker or the slots. Walk into any casino and you will see people competing at each and every one of the games I listed. Personally, I prefer sports betting, poker, Pai Gow poker, craps, roulette, and video poker in that order. I love blackjack but it is an unbeatable game. If you are reading this book on slots, then obviously that is your game of choice. So be it.

I've already explained what you are up against, but then there are barriers that the casinos have going for them in every game. The professional player at his game of choice has increased his chances of winning by becoming a perfect player at his particular game. The pro also has a fabulous, unrelenting, controlled, never yielding handle on discipline, which cuts losses to the bone.

I've given you loss limits and naked pulls to cut your losses. I've told you to accept small wins in slots play. Now it's up to you to become that perfect player at slots. Should you play the slots? Hey, if that's your game, go to it, but heed my advice!

The answer for the last chapter is 3,200,000 possible combinations for a five-reel, twenty-symbol machine. (Good guess.)

24

Wrapping Up Knowledge

Well, thank God this section is over. It's just that there is only so much you can say about knowledge of the game, when it comes to slots, that it becomes a series of boring chapters. But at least I was able to get across the importance of:

1. Knowing there is a little chip that isn't exactly player friendly.

2. Realizing that your bankroll determines whether you play nickel, quarter, or dollar slots.

3. What the chances are against us every time we approach those beautifully decorated but potentially coin-eating machines.

It is a Friday morning in a cold, windy (as usual) January in New Jersey. I will be leaving on my almost daily two-and-a-half-hour trip to Atlantic City. It's a long ride on a toll-infested parkway, where coupled with the price of gas, to keep the car running for those more than 200 miles, the expenses are close to $20 before I reach my first table.

The aisles are jammed with people who arrive by bus for their day at the casinos and it is usually the seniors who will gather in the slot and video-poker sections. Many of them recognize me from my TV shows and videos and come over to chat. The main question from the machine players is always the same, "Can you win at these monsters?" My answer is always the same, "Only if you'll accept small wins and learn to quit with small profits."

I then tell them that the best games to play, in order are: poker, Pai Gow poker, baccarat, craps, roulette, video poker, Let It Ride, slots and blackjack. But so many of them are intimidated by the table games that they are scared to learn the games. If you are in that category, at least attack the machine family with a couple of the methods I will lay out in the next section.

Armed with a few of these money-management moves, plus the loss limits and naked-pull advice we already went over—you will have a shot.

Finally, and I have said this before: if machine play is your bag, give a look to video poker. I play it every day.

Since it is in the machine family, all the advice and money management methods coming up next can be applied, because it is all in the same family—or have I said that before? And now on to the best part in the book: Money Management!

PART IV

Money Management

25

Money Management

Now we get to the key to every gambling venture ever attempted. This is the third part of the Big Four and tied with discipline as the most important. You've all heard of money management and everyone has a different explanation of what it actually is and what it means. None of those theories are wrong, but let me put the whole process into one simple phrase, "Money management is knowing what to bet after a win and what to bet after a loss."

You don't have to be a Rhodes scholar to decipher that sentence. But you gotta be one strong cat to set up that series and follow it to a "T."

I live and breathe by a betting method called the "regression system," which is aimed at play for table games, such as baccarat, roulette, blackjack, Pai Gow, and craps. It is a method whereby your first bet is higher than the table minimum and if you win that bet, you regress to the minimum, putting you in a no-lose situation. For example, you are at a $5 blackjack table.

1. First bet $10 (or $6, $7, $8 or $9, as long as it is higher than $5).

2. Say you win that first bet (example $10).

3. Take back the $10 first bet and $5 of the $10 payoff and bet $5.

4. You have recouped the original $10 bet and a $5 profit and have a $5 wager for the next hand.

5. Even if you lose that second bet, you are ahead $5 for that series.

6. You won a hand, lost a hand, the same as the dealer (you played the house even), and still showed a profit.

Now that method is geared to even-money or practically even-money games (like placing 6 and 8 in craps), and not geared to the slots or video poker. But it is money management and I *never* veer from it, throughout my table play. When I head to the machines, and I've already totally endorsed playing video poker, I have several betting series that I follow religiously. I never deviate even one single coin when following the series I laid out, before I even sit at a machine.

There will be several of these methods laid out for you in this section. Some you will like, some you won't. You are free to grab the theory of a method of betting and add your own moves, whether they are aggressive or conservative. But the important thing is that you *do* have a predetermined betting series in place at every machine.

Money management is simply, "Knowing what to bet . . "

Oh, go back and read the beginning of the chapter!

26

Do You Want Money Management?

Probably not! Yeah, you'll say you want it, have it, or think about it, or some such nonsense, but do you honestly and truthfully wanna approach gambling with the most important tool required?

I think I heard a couple of *nos!* Probably came from my friends, Les Branes and Enna Fogg. These people have no clue as to the importance of a controlled approach to gambling, regardless of what game you play.

People tell me every day that they go to the casinos with intentions of following a controlled method of betting. At the table games you will see these people betting the exact amount of chips hand after hand. That is called "flat betting." They bet $5 every single hand, whether they win or lose the previous hand. This is also true at craps and roulette and it is done by people who don't grasp the power of trends. They fail to increase their wagers when they are winning, and obviously fail to be able to cash in when things are going their way.

Then of course there are those that increase their wagers when they are losing, figuring their play is due to change and they wanna be betting high, when it is their *turn* to win. Ridiculous thinking, a lack of comprehension of trends, and the unwillingness to vary bets will beat the uncontrolled player every time. But these people really don't want controls. Of course they don't like losing but they still don't wanna do the things that you *must* do to avoid losing.

It's not uncommon for someone to say to me, "I know you're right about discipline and money management, but once I get to the tables or at the machines, I get all fired up with the action and figure I'll use discipline the next time."

Actually it's up to each individual player to decide if he or she wants to take the trouble of becoming a strong player. Because that's exactly what it's going to take for you to change your approach.

You bought this book because you obviously wanted to learn a few things about gambling. Well, I'm telling you right now that if you don't use money management, even at the slot machines, you're just throwing money down the drain.

I'm gonna take all the fun out of your haphazard way of playing and show you how to play the slots with a measure of intelligence. Whether you wanna pay attention or not is strictly up to you. I'll repeat the question that was posted as the title of this chapter and see what your answer is.

"Do you want money management?" If you said no, close the book. If you said yes, let's move on.

27

Systems in Slots

I hate the word system when it comes to gambling. It always seems like the person giving out the system is just such a snake-oil salesman and has a wonder drug for sale. So instead of calling my suggestions "systems," I'm gonna refer to them as "methods of betting." That is exactly what they are. (But, I will call them systems, as I lay out their pros and cons.)

I am going to give you a few ideas of how to bet at these machines. You may like the approaches or you may laugh at them. Whatever you do, don't totally discount their value. I'll be talking about the quarter machines, but if you like the higher bets, merely adjust your thinking to the amount of coins you will be betting.

You won't (can't) win every time. That's impossible. But you will have days when you get ahead and then must come the decision, from you, as to whether you wanna quit with that small profit or take the chance of blowing back that profit.

So how do you get ahead at the machines? Well, I'd be lying if I told you that by using systems, you'll get ahead constantly. That is simply not true.

The method of betting, with controlled series, is a two-pronged theory that the novice gambler just doesn't grasp:

1. Method betting allows you to bet smaller when losing.
2. Method betting allows you to bet higher when winning.

Maybe that doesn't seem important to you, but it is a key to winning. By betting smaller at cold or choppy machines, it prevents you from falling so far behind that even a decent winning machine won't allow you to recoup your losses, which became too steep with stupid overbetting.

In the next chapter we will start with a bunch of betting methods that you may or may not like. Pick a few and try them out. There is also nothing wrong with you adding a wrinkle or two! It is also important that you don't plan on using four to six different systems on any given day.

That thinking would have you popping back and forth, not giving any of them a decent chance to see if they are working. *One or two* methods of play a day is enough. So even though I refer to the dreaded word "system," when it is in reality a method of betting, I will bounce back and forth in my terminology, to keep both "method" and "system" lovers happy. First, I will show you methods of play for 3-coin machines, then I will show you methods for 5-coin machines.

28

System 1: Up the Steps

This is my favorite, so why not start off with it? It ain't like I'm gonna save the plum for the end to make you keep waiting for the grand finale. Of course there are spinoffs for the basic play, but the name gives off the theory: "up the steps."

At a 3-coin machine you start at the lowest step (1 or 2 coins) and move up the steps, as you pick up wins. If the machine is *not* kicking off wins then you remain at the lowest step.

Again, and I repeat the word *again,* so I get your attention, my systems can be applied to both the slots and the video poker machines, because we are dealing with similar betting devices.

We will start with slots: The word jackpot is erroneously embellished in the minds of most slots players. They wanna win the jackpot. Go back to the chapter where I showed you the tremendous amount of possible combinations that are available and how tough it is to win the jackpot.

So by constantly banging in max coins at a 3-coin machine, you stand the chance of trying to catch a flying feather in a thimble, especially with a short bankroll. So with that in mind, let us say you take $10 to a machine and start with 1 coin. If you lose, bet 1 coin, lose, 1 coin, lose, 1 coin, lose, 1 coin. You are betting the minimum and staying there because of no return. Don't forget, you have a 60 percent loss limit on that $10 and we'll say a naked-pull number of ten.

Finally, on the sixth pull, you get a return. Now you go up to 2 coins and if you win at 2 coins, move to 3. If you increased to 2 coins after that first win and lost with that 2-coin play, back you go to 1 coin.

This is the basic premise of "Up the Steps" play. You stay at the base level until it kicks off a return. If you win at level one and go to level two, where you immediately win again, then you shoot up to level three, which in this case is max coins. If you win at level three, you stay there and continue betting max coins; regardless of the payoff, even one cherry for a 3-coin return.

When you lose at level three, you drop to level two. If you win at level two, go to level 3. If you lose at level two, drop to level one.

Get the idea? You're betting small when losing, increasing when winning. Hold that thought!

29

System 2: Up the Steps: High/Low

You have the basic play of this system. Now let's look at some options you can include. We're still talking about three-reel slots, so don't start thinking about the five-reel machines just yet. First, I want you to completely grasp the theory of up the steps.

In the previous chapter we started at 1 coin and progressed only after a win. But that increase was one step at a time. We would start at level one and go to level two after a return and then to max coins of level three after that next win.

In this scenario, called high/low, our betting amounts are restricted to just 1 coin (minimum) and 3 coins (maximum). In this case, there is no stopping at level two, but the idea of increasing our bets remains constant. We go up only after a win. The difference is that the jump is from 1 coin to 3 (max). If we get a return at max coins, we stay there. If we get to level three and lose the 3-coin play, back we go to level one and start all over.

Our naked pulls and loss limits remain the same. Plus, the temptation to increase bets, before a return is realized, is out of the question. Stay right there at level one until you see that credit total on your machine start to increase. Yeah, there will still be the weeping and gnashing of teeth about a jackpot occurring while you are betting single coins.

How come these same people don't bellyache as much when they put in 3 coins and get zilch?

The "up the steps" method has loads more options when we get to 5-coin play, but right now, content yourself with understanding the power of:

1. Cutting losses.
2. Accepting small returns.

Pretty soon you'll love the concept because you'll understand it.

30

System 3: Patterns

Obviously, there are both conservative and aggressive gamblers at every game in the casino. At the craps table you'll find the players who love to press (increase) their bets in the blink of an eye. Players like me, very conservative in their approach, prefer to grind out small returns in a more consistent manner.

I have found conservative play more rewarding. The big paydays are not quite as constant but the big loss days are very, very rare. The aggressive players do end up with high paydays on occasion but also get their chains rattled to the tune of big losses on days when things ain't going so well.

The "up the steps" approach is very popular with us conservative players, but maybe you crave a little more aggressive play. I call this "pattern play," because the increases are not predicated on a winning pull, rather a predetermined pattern of bets that you set up ahead of time.

You can choose any pattern you like but it has to be set up before you venture onto the casino floor. Otherwise you'll be making wild bets and decisions on hunches, feelings, or any other gut feeling that enters your mind.

Let's say you set up a betting sequence, geared to a series of fifteen bets: 1-1-1-2-2-2-3-3-3-2-2-2-1-1-1. In this case you have set 27 coins aside to play out this pattern. There is no loss limit or naked pull amount to stop you. You pick a machine and go through with the pattern. If, when the series is complete, you have back your original investment plus a profit, then you rat-hole these extra coins and go through the same 27-coin series again. I use a 50 percent loss limit in a series to gear my stay at a machine. If I lose three consecutive series of 14 or more coins, then that session (machine) is complete.

You do not change the predetermined pattern at any machine. If you started with the one I laid out (27), then you play it out that way for every series you attempt at that particular machine. When a 27-coin series is complete, I always put aside the profits and play only the series set up ahead of time.

You can stay at a machine as long as you keep winning, *but,* and this is where you gotta keep records, you do not stay at a machine if:

1.   You lose three series in a row.

2.   You lose three out of four series.

Now let's also be smart about this, without my standing there in back of you, to make sure you don't fall in love with a machine.

Suppose you lose 16 coins, lose 14 coins, win 6 coins, lose 12 coins, win 3 coins—you're being ground out, even though there were not three consecutive losing sessions.

Leave that machine!

31

System 4: Aggressive Patterns

OK, still staying with the pattern method, let's set it up to let you play a little more aggressively. The only thing to remember is that you can't just increase the amount of your bets, just because you want to. The pattern series I laid out for you in the previous chapter was based on $10 session money. If you double your series, you have to go up at least 50 percent on the money you bring to that machine.

My friend Penny Pincher loves the casino life but hates gambling. She just doesn't wanna lose her money at the machines and she is right. Penny brings six pennies, fourteen nickels, a handful of dimes, and two rolls of quarters to the machine. She does not have the right (or brains) to bet the way my friend Lotta Kash can play. Lotta has $100 a session and can well afford to lay out big series.

Be sure you stay within the intelligent controls of your bankroll. Ten dollars per session is acceptable for basic series but in the ones I'll lay out here, you should raise your session money accordingly. Here's an example of upping your series:

- 2-2-2-3-3-3-2-2-2-3-3-3-2-2-2   You'll note that this is a planned play of 36 coins, so bringing just a roll of quarters is not suggested (which is 40 coins).

I'd prefer that you bring 60 coins for that size pattern. I would also suggest raising your pattern series only after you have had a couple of winning series at the lower level. In other words, start off at a machine using the basic, low betting pattern. If you leave that machine with a profit, then you can take a shot with higher bets. Why would you suffer through three or four losing machines and then suddenly go to a higher series, just because you wanna recoup your losses? Remember *trends* and wait for one to develop in your favor. If you do make a profit then you can try these next two problems:

- 2-2-3-3-3-2-2-3-3-3-2-2
- 2-3-3-2-3-3-2-3-3-2-3-3

With number 1, you're playing 30 coins and with number 2 you're playing 32 coins. Both of these series should have a minimum of 60 coins per session.

With three-reel slot machines, you are restricted somewhat in the amount of series that you can set up. But I definitely wouldn't suggest playing the same amount or max coins, play after play.

I occasionally play patterns, but they are always geared to having minimum bets along the way such as:

- 1-2-1-3-1-2-1-3-1-2-1-3.

That's 21 coins and well within the use of a roll of quarters. Don't forget, you can always increase your bets when you get ahead.

One adjustment I just have to suggest. I said you didn't need naked pulls, but if you go ten to twelve straight zippo's, don't you think it would be nice to be able to walk from that frigid machine? Then do it! That machine is cold!

32

System 5: Controlled Pattern

Do you get the idea by now, that slots play isn't just putting coins into a machine and hoping (and praying). It is all *money management*. I gave you a theory that I like, up the steps, and another that I play occasionally; it is a pattern series, where you lay out a series of bets before you even enter the casino.

With the pattern, you are occasionally betting max coins, in the hope of catching lightning in a bottle. In other words, you could hit a semi-jackpot and get paid a decent amount of coins because the pattern play has you varying your bets.

With the "up the steps" method, you could be playing minimum coins when the big hit comes and get merely a small payoff because of the fact you were betting small. Those situations don't bother me, because I am more concerned with cutting losses and not getting whacked at subcold machines.

You have to decide which betting methods you like best, but whichever ones you settle on, *please*, at least have some sort of controlled play. Every day I see people playing max coins and the looks on their faces cannot mask the disappointment that engulfs them as their bankrolls swiftly diminish. Don't constantly play max coins. Adopt either the "up the steps" theory (betting small when losing) or adopting some type of similar theory.

Just for smiles, we'll go for one more look at a pattern, but this time it is controlled by a naked-pull number, which I will put at ten, but you can change if you like. Try this:

- 1-2-3-3-2-1-1-2-3-3-2-1

That one has only 24 total coins at risk, if you go for the whole series, so you can't get hurt. Plus, you have four shots at max coins, plus you have your naked pulls to protect you. If you don't like the up the steps and the pattern tickles your fancy—give this series your initial shot.

That's it for pattern play. You either like it—or you don't.

33

System 6: The Chicken System

This method is everything the title suggests. You're gonna play only one session at a machine, then run like a chicken, whether ahead or behind.

Your bankroll is broken into sessions, we'll say $20 is your designated amount per machine on this day. You will take that amount to a machine of your choosing and pick a series of bets that you like.

It could be any of the ones we went over, or one that you have invented, with its own built-in series:

1. Up the steps
2. Pattern 1-1-2-2-3-3-2-2-1-1
3. Pattern 2-3-2-3-2-3-2-3

The choice of series is yours, plus there is no loss-limit or naked-pull restriction with this system. You are taking a shot at a machine, whereby at the conclusion of you inserting the entire amount of that session amount, you clear out the credits and run like a chicken: Win or lose!

I have hinted throughout this book that the little chip is not in our corner. It is a fact that many people believe that once a machine, whether it be a slot or video-poker variety, has hit a big payoff, it suddenly goes frigid.

I am also one of those who believes this to be true. Whether it is or not, will never be determined, but many times, you will see a player immediately cash out their chips, as soon as a big payoff occurs.

Good for them. I have seen many times with my play, where this happens, so I give that machine a few more bets, wait for five naked pulls and leave if nothing is happening. The chicken system predetermines that you will leave as soon as your session is completed.

My friend Watt E. Cey is questioning what I said, because it goes against my principles of never leaving a machine that is kicking off profits.

Well, the chicken takes that into consideration, plus the fact that machines also (mysteriously) enter into prolonged dry spells. The chicken has these rules:

1. Take the session amount.
2. Decide on a series and betting amount.
3. Leave the machine when all coins are deposited.
4. There are no naked pulls or loss limits.
5. Leave when the session amount is completed with your profit or loss.

NOTE: Since I never leave a machine on a winning play, because it may be the start of a hot trend—there is one *but!*

If the last play of your session amount is a win, keep playing until you lose a bet. *Never* leave if the last play is a winning one. Will you like the chicken? I dunno, but as far as systems go, it sure ain't a turkey! Man, am I sorry I said that!

34

System 7: The Squirrel System

This is a method that incorporates the moves of a squirrel. You know, they grab food and squirrel (hide) it away for a future time. It is their idea of building up on excess (profit) to be utilized down the line.

Well, the "squirrel system" can be adjusted as part of the chicken. We'll say you took $20 to a machine to play the chicken and set up a pattern play of 1-2-3-3-2-1-1-2-3-3-2-1 as the series.

Finally you catch a pretty decent machine that stays hot throughout the session. At the conclusion of your play, you have your $20 (80 credits) showing, plus another 70 credits, meaning you had a great run.

We know the chicken has you grabbing your booty and running. However, if you predetermined to go from a chicken to a squirrel (you oughta make a ton of money if you patent that move), then you don't leave that machine.

Take the $20 (80 credits) you started with and rat-hole them. You have your investment back. Now take the 70 credits remaining:

1. Put half (35 coins) away, meaning you are *guaranteed* to leave that machine a bonafide winner.

2. Take the remaining 35 coins (your excess) and run another series at *that* machine.

3. This squirrel method keeps you at a good machine.

Now, when that second series run is completed, you repeat the process:

1. If you have less than the amount of coins you started with (35 in this case), that session is over and you leave the machine.

2. If you have increased that amount, we'll say you now have 75 credits, an increase of 40 coins, you stay at that machine.

3. Take the 40-coin profit and break it in half. Put 50 percent (20 coins) with your guarantee and add the other 20 coins (50 percent) to the 35 for that session. You now have 55 coins for a new session.

4. Run a new session with your 55 coins.

When that session is complete, you leave if you have less than 55. If you have over 55, repeat the scenario I laid out for you.

This squirrel method keeps you playing at a machine that is staying hot. Don't skip the next chapter. This theory is going to go into depth. But take a look at this squirrel system. You won't be nuts if it becomes part of your day. Man, I don't know why I said that—again!

Incidentally, you'll notice I give you examples that are very close to minimum play but that is because I am talking to those with limited bankrolls.

But the *theory* remains the same. If you play higher amounts, merely keep the same thought but adjust, according to your own personal wins and losses.

35

Guarantee and Excess

Notice how I add this theory right into the book when the squirrel method is fresh in your mind? That's because they are both
from the same family. They can be (and should be) utilized,
regardless of what casino game you play.

Veterans of my theories, which are in every one of my books
and videos, know what the move guarantee and excess will do to
their money-management approach. When you complete a session
at the table games, craps, blackjack, roulette, etc., you don't wanna
exit a table that has been good to you. For instance, you are playing craps and a hot shooter has just completed a roll that allows
you to comfortably exceed your win goal. You don't wanna leave
that table, yet you believe in applying discipline, getting to your
win goal and not giving back the profits. OK, enter guarantee and
excess:

1. Take your starting session money and rat-hole it.

2. Take your craps profits for that table, we'll say $100 and
   break it in half.

3. Fifty dollars (half) goes in your pocket, never to be touched
   again that day. It's called your guarantee.

4. $50 (the other half) is now your excess amount for staying at
   that hot table.

5. You are content that your starting session amount is safely tucked away.

6. You're content that you have a guaranteed $50 tucked away, making you a winner for that session.

7. You're content because even if you lose the excess, you are still a winner for that session.

With that new $50 excess session, every new shooter should be considered a separate move. Let's say, after the next shooter completes his roll, you have won another $22.

Now you put half ($11) with your guarantee, increasing that amount of profit and add the other half ($11) to your $50 session amount, giving you $61 to continue playing. Continue making this move for every subsequent shooter. When you lose two shooters in a row, that session is *fini!*

Add what is left of that excess to your guarantee and leave that table. Once you hit your original win goal, all the subsequent moves simply put you in fat city. For you people just getting involved in slots play, I merely took the guarantee and excess theory, called it the "squirrel" and applied it to your play at slots. This is a very important part of your day. The squirrel should not be used with the chicken, but with any session you compete at.

Don't be a pig in gambling. Get in the habit of setting aside small profits. Man, with all the points made, alluding to a chicken, squirrel, and pig—maybe you oughta just start a farm!

36

System 8: The Three-Star System

The "three-star system" is geared to 3-coin machines and uses a bunch of long series to play a session. The three-star system incorporates a variation on the theory of naked pulls called "naked numbers." While naked pulls limits your losses and signifies the end to a session at a machine, "naked numbers" limits your losses by signifying the end to a level of a series. For instance, you are playing a series that reads: 3-3-3-3-3-3-3-3-3-3-2-2-2-2-2-2-2-2-2-2-1-1-1-1-1-1-1-1-1-1. That's ten pulls per coin level. You set a naked number of four, which means if you are playing 3 coins and you get four empty pulls, you drop down to the next lowest amount and play 2 coins for ten straight pulls. So if you have four empty pulls, you don't end the session but you do drop one betting level and continue the series at that level. Let's give that a quick review:

1. Naked Pulls: When you start a session, this is the number you set to end the session and leave that machine. It should be between seven and fourteen empty pulls. Whatever number you feel most comfortable with.

2. Naked Number: When you play a series that calls for a long amount of pulls at a certain level, the idea is to reduce the number of pulls at that amount so as not to get hurt. You

choose the number depending on the length of the series, but it should be between 30 percent and 50 percent of the length of the series.

The naked number theory is an excellent tool that allows you to stay at a certain machine, but gives you a chance to drop to a lower bet. Just be sure to keep an eye on your loss limits and naked pulls that signal the end of that session. You don't wanna set your naked pulls at eight and then exceed that limit just because you are dropping to a lower level; and you never exceed your loss limit. If you set a loss limit at 50 percent don't keep playing just because the series isn't yet over. A loss limit is just that: a limit.

I live and die by the application of discipline and a conservative approach to gambling. Naked numbers, along with naked pulls and loss limits, are powerful keys. Please get to understand them and, pretty please, *use them.*

With the three-star method you use ten bets per level. You need to have a $20 session amount for quarter slot machines and a $30 session amount for half-dollar machines. Remember you have to break up your bankroll into realistic sessions and set loss limits. Here are some examples of the three-star system:

- 1-1-1-1-1-1-1-1-1-1-2-2-2-2-2-2-2-2-2-2-3-3-3-3-3-3-3-3-3-3-3-2-2-2-2-2-2-2-2-2-2-3-3-3-3-3-3-3-3-3-3-1-1-1-1-1-1-1-1-1-1.

- 2-2-2-2-2-2-2-2-2-2-1-1-1-1-1-1-1-1-1-1-2-2-2-2-2-2-2-2-2-2-3-3-3-3-3-3-3-3-3-3-2-2-2-2-2-2-2-2-2-2-1-1-1-1-1-1-1-1-1-1-2-2-2-2-2-2-2-2-2-2-3-3-3-3-3-3-3-3-3-3.

- 3-3-3-3-3-3-3-3-3-3-2-2-2-2-2-2-2-2-2-2-1-1-1-1-1-1-1-1-1-1-3-3-3-3-3-3-3-3-3-3-2-2-2-2-2-2-2-2-2-2-1-1-1-1-1-1-1-1-1-1.

Just to go over this system, I like the fact that there are ten pulls at each level with protection coming from the addition of naked numbers. Let's say nine was the naked pulls you set and the naked number was four.

1. If you have nine naked pulls the session is over, so you're protected against a disaster.

2. If you have four empty pulls in a row, you've reached your naked number and drop to the next lowest level. This cuts down a heavy insertion of coins at a high level on a cold machine.

You can add optional moves to the three-star system. My favorite move is jumping the bet to a higher level when a win occurs. I believe that move should be incorporated into most methods because of the logical theory that you want to take advantage of streaks or trends.

With the three-star system you have another option move when you jump to a higher level:

1. You can stay at the level you jumped to and complete that line.

2. You can slide back to the level you jumped from when a loss occurs.

I prefer number 1 since that keeps you at a higher level of play and ensures a nice return if the machine stays hot. You then can pick up the series you predetermined.

The three-star system is one that I like, and I think you will, too. You may wanna use it the way I laid it out or you may wanna add a twist or two to it.

37

System 9: The Simple System

I've saved the easiest system for last because even though all of you people wanna win, only about 30 percent of you believe that you should have a money-management method for playing slots. Of that 30 percent, only about a dozen of you will actually follow these strict money-control methods. That's because you really haven't grasped the true reality of gambling and how tough it is to win.

My friend Don Beeleave doesn't believe that anything I say about money management can help him at the slots. After reading all the systems, his reasons for not following them include:

1. They're too time-consuming.
2. They're too much trouble.
3. It gives him a headache trying to remember the systems.
4. They prevent him from winning jackpots most of the time. (He hasn't won one yet in twenty-three years of playing slots.)
5. He doesn't like moving to different machines so much.
6. He believes you should only play max coins all the time, even if your bankroll is only $30.
7. He doesn't know why he doesn't like the approach, can't think of a good reason to knock it, but knocks it anyhow, just on principle.

Maybe you don't believe in systems, just like Don Beeleave, but you'd better realize that the only way you're gonna grind out consistent returns is by controlling your money and reducing losses. But enough of that, here's the final 3-coin system and we'll call it the "simple system" (pretty original, huh?).

We'll say you have a small bankroll, perhaps $100, and wanna spend the day in the casino. You accept the fact that you have a small bankroll and you accept the fact that you'll accept a nice 30 percent or 40 percent return on your session money. I'll accept that acceptance because it is intelligent.

Set your naked pulls, let's say nine, and set your loss limits and win goals at 60 percent. You'll take $5, which is 20 coins, to the machine. You will always start at the middle bet, which in this case is 2 coins. (You can play this system on a 5-coin machine as well, where you would start at 3 coins.) Here's how simple it is:

1. Insert 2 coins.
2. If you win on the first pull, jump to max coins.
3. Stay at max coins as long as you keep getting winning pulls.
4. As soon as a loss occurs, you drop one level.
5. Each time you win, you always jump to max coins.
6. A loss only calls for a drop of one level.
7. Once you get to 1 coin, you stay there if you keep losing.
8. You play until you lose nine in a row (or whatever naked-pull number you set).
9. There is no naked number for this system, only naked pulls and loss limits.
10. Your loss limit is 60 percent. In the case of a $5 session, this would be $3.
11. You go to max coins after a win and stay there as you win. You drop one level after each loss.

How can you get a simpler system than the simple system? This is a particularly good system for people with short bankrolls. I gave you a session amount of $5 per session, but if you like, you can make it $10 with a loss limit reduced to 40 percent or 50 percent.

I really like the simple system because it is restrictive; it is hard to get hurt badly with this method. Then again it keeps you into acceptance of a 60 percent return and then reverting to the use of guarantee and excess. Try the simple system!

38

Reviewing Systems

I've just laid out nine systems of betting that can be applied to the three-reel slot machines. Naturally, you are encouraged to look over these moves and add your own wrinkles. It's pretty hard to give a lot of variations for the three-reel machine but you absolutely, positively must have a controlled betting series or else you're just dumping money down the drain. We'll take a thumbnail glance at each method, just to refresh your memory.

Up the Steps: This is my favorite, mostly because I can bet small when losing and betting max at the hottest times. This method gets another look at five-reel machines.

High/Low: This is in the "up the steps" family, but a freckle more aggressive because you can jump from min to max play in a blink, so for good reason I like this play.

Pattern Bets: Not a bad approach because it fosters discipline. The drawback is that you may be locked into low betting series when the machine is hot. The good part is its control over losses. Don't discard the theory.

Chicken System: Good start-up system for clueless players (those with refusal to adhere to discipline). The theory keeps you moving by adding in the squirrel move. Don't push this one onto the back burner.

Squirrel System: Actually, the method is geared to the chicken method, but can be adapted to any system you decide to play. It's a godchild of the guarantee and excess theory but until you completely understand it, at least come up with some plan of salting away profits.

The Three-Star System: This method uses a bunch of long series to play a session. There are ten pulls at each level, but it has a built-in safeguard called "naked numbers," whereby if you have a number of empty pulls in a row, you drop down to the next lowest betting level.

The Simple System: You start with a middle bet (2 coins). If you win you jump to max coins. You stay at max coins until a loss occurs, then you drop one betting level. After every loss you drop one level; after every win you jump to max bets, simple right?

Take a few minutes to examine each of these plays and see where you can add a wrinkle. There are good points with each, that will protect your play.

Next chapter we switch to reviewing the five-reel machines, which also can apply to the 5-coin video poker machines.

39

Five-Reel Machines

The way casinos are adding and subtracting the various slot machines on the floor, this book may be obsolete before it gets printed. In every casino I enter, there are sections roped off where old models are replaced by newer versions.

Well, it is the year 2001 and I will address the machines that are in action right now. We've already touched on three-reelers. Let's take a look at the five-reel babies. Obviously, the more reels, the more symbols; the more symbols, the more combinations; the more combinations, the less chance of winning; the less chance of winning, the harder it is on the player. The harder it is on the player is directly associated with there being more reels. Did you get all that? I get the feeling I was talking in circles. But if I was, it was because it always goes around and around, and comes back to where the paying customers get it—in the pocketbook.

I'll be leaving for A.C. in about two hours and will play some Pai-Gow poker, seven-card stud poker, craps and finish with about $100 allocated to video poker. I always buy in with $40, which is 160 coins (quarters), per session. I play at the Jacks or Better and Double Joker machines. I set win goals and naked pulls and above all: loss limit.

Right across the aisles from me are the slots players, pouring their coins into the one-armed bandits. And most of them are playing max coins. With max play at these 5-coin sponges, you can have your money sucked up pretty quickly at a cold machine.

I have more money than many of the people playing the max. So why don't I play the full amount all the time? Because that is a stupid way to play! Oops, I guess I could have been a little more diplomatic in my assessment of others, but if the truth be told— Now if you wanna dance with wolves, go ahead. But if you get into a method of play that will limit your losses and give you a shot at picking up small consistent wins, then I suggest you hang on my every word.

Again, I will say it, because people like my friend Watt E. Cey will say, "I don't remember you saying that." This book is on *slots,* but the theories, while pointed to the slots players can also be applied to video poker and any subsequent machines, on any subject, blackjack for instance, that requires 5-coin play.

Keep that in mind as we start the methods of betting for 5-coin machines.

40

System 10: 5-Coin Up the Steps

You don't need me to explain the theory of this play because I went over the basic moves, when discussing its use at 3-coin machines. The fact that we have moved to 5-coin machines and wanna use this method, merely means that it opens a load of variations of bets.

I told you that I use the "up the steps" betting moves every day. I love the idea of:

1. Bet small when losing.
2. Increase bets when winning.

It is in the same family as:

1. Drink water when you're thirsty.
2. Don't drink if you're not thirsty.

Do you understand the connection? If not, then you didn't grasp the message with the second part of the Little Three—logic!

Your assignment for tonight: Write the word "logic" 1,000 times, or at least until you see how logical it is to:

1. Bet low when losing.
2. Bet high *only* when winning.

Or have I said that before?

Here are some ideas for use at a 5-coin machine. (Excuse the use of the word "I," but in all honesty, this is the way I play. So it is easier to get my point across by the use of that word.)

1. I buy in with $40, which equates to 160 coins.
2. This gives me a decent amount of plays.
3. The first three bets are 3 coins each, based on the fact that *if* a machine is hot, I start off with a nice run.
4. I *never* play from credits, instead I drop all coins from my buy-in into the tray.
5. I then manually insert coins, depending on amount required for that play.
6. Yes, I need a lot of Handi Wipes and trips to the men's room to wash my hands.
7. If I don't hit in the first three plays, I revert to a 2-coin bet.
8. I *never* bet 1 coin at a 5-coin machine. Two is the minimum, 3 is usual, 4 is *never*, 5 (max) when I hit at 3.
9. After regressing to 2-coin play, I stay there, as long as no return shows.
10. When a win (any return) shows at 2, I immediately go to 3-coin play.
11. If I win at 3, I go to 5. If loss occurred at 3, I drop back to 2.
12. When I get to 5-coin play, I stay there for only one play, and win or lose, go back to 3-coin play.

NOTE: OK, read number 12 again. You may want, when you get to max play and win, to stay there for another max play. That is your option. I prefer to go back to 3 coins.

13. If I win at 3 (after dropping back from level five), I again go back to 5.
14. A loss at 3 coins and I'm back to 2.

Before jumping to the next chapter, go back over these lucky fourteen steps. (I didn't say if they were lucky for you or the casino!)

41

System 11: Options

Let's stay with system 10 and revisit those fourteen steps of betting. Maybe you agree with them or maybe you'd like to add a wrinkle or two. The total concept lies with the fact that my key number is right in the middle—level three. I start there and use the flow at that machine to either drop me to 2 coins or raise me to 5. Before you ask the typical query, which my friend Jack Pott, is itching to put to me, let me answer it.

Question: What if you hit the jackpot with only 2 coins?

Answer: I don't even blink. Just like I don't blink when I bet 5 coins and get a zippo return. (Well, that does tick me off, but that wasn't the question!)

There are many people like Jack Pott, who have only jackpots on their minds when they play the machines.

As I speak, it is a Friday in February and I have already been to the casinos three times this week. I played the video poker machines for a time each day and on Wednesday, at the Showboat Casino, at a Jacks or Better machine, I was in the middle of a series (exactly as I just laid out). I bet 3 coins (*not* 5), because I had gotten a push, one pair, on the previous play and could not go to max play. I was dealt in this order: AD, KD, QD, 4D, 5S. I held the first three (yes, I killed the 4D), and up popped: AD, KD,

QD, JD, 10D (in that order). I got 750 coins for my 3-coin play. Did I blink because I didn't have 5 coins in? No, but I did blink when the cocktail waitress in that section heard the bells and came over to congratulate me. She makes Dolly Parton look like a boy, but that's another story.

I was ecstatic to win with 3 coins and the fraction of an instant that you realize that it is more important to *not* bet max coins all the time, is the moment you become an aware player.

A couple of "buts" to the fourteen steps is in order here. If you agree with my theory, good—*but* if you'd like to change some things, here are suggestions:

1. When I bet 3 coins and win, I go to 5 coins, *but* . . .

2. If I push at 3 coins, get my money back with one pair, I stay at 3 coins, *but* . .

3. If I am at 2 coins and push, get my money back with one pair, I do go to 3 coins.

Notice the *buts?* A 2-coin push calls for a jump to 3. *But* a 3-coin push does *not* call for a jump to 5. I don't bet 1 coin on 5-coin machines because of the minimal return, so that level is out. However, if you have a session amount of only $10, then, by all means, use that level.

I also never bet 4, but go right from 3 to 5 coins. Again, your session money dictates whether you should do the same or take a more conservative series approach.

42

System 12: Smaller Steps

Back in the bankroll section I mentioned that your economic situation dictated the amount of each session. Then that session amount dictated the size of your bets. I play with 160 coins per session and use the bets of 2, 3, or 5 exclusively. That is not to say that a person with 40 coins ($10) should play that way. It also does not say that a person with a $60 (240-coin) buy-in should adopt my play either. He could eliminate the 1, 2, and 4 levels and stay with 3 and 5.

I feel comfortable with my series and use it only as an example, so that you can use it as a guide to gauge how you will set up your series. We'll take the case of a buy-in of $10 (40 coins) for a machine. Here are some suggestions:

1. Start at 2 coins for three plays.
2. If, after three plays, you have no return, drop to 1 coin.
3. As long as you get zippo return (up to your naked pull number), stay at 1 coin.
4. When you get a hit, go back to 2 coins.
5. If a loss shows, drop back to 1 coin.
6. If a win occurs at the second level, go up to the third level.
7. If a loss comes at that third level, you have two options:

    a. Drop to 1 coin.

    b. Drop to 2 coins. But definitely drop.

8. If a win shows at the third level, you have three choices:

   a. Go to 4 coins.

   b. Go to 5 coins.

   c. Stay at the third level. You may want to stay at that level for another shot.

9. If you went to the fourth level with a win at 3 coins, a win at 4 would shoot you to max play.

10. When you get to max play, you have several options:

   a. A loss drops you either 1, 2, or 3 levels.

   b. A win either keeps you at 5 or drops you to the third level.

   c. A win could drop you to the second level and then go back over the previous suggestions for plays, depending on a win or loss.

These are just a few of the options open to you at each level and depend on the result. It is not only important but *imperative* that you have laid out your decisions prior to your playing.

Every single solitary move (bet) I make is predetermined. Do I get tempted to bet higher, after a three-four-five run of blanks? You bet your life I do—but I don't. I don't know if that last sentence is grammatically correct, but logically it is right on the button.

I love the "up the steps" method, whether it is with the use of one step or two steps at a time. It all depends on your bankroll—or have I said that before?

43

System 13: Low/High

Again, I've already given you the high/low theory at 3 coins, so you can slide right into this theory, as it applies to a 5-coin machine. You have the option of using a spread bet between 2 coins/5 coins or 3 coins/5 coins. There is nothing in between in either case.

Loss limits and naked pulls are required but the basic premise of this betting method is very clear:

1. You're betting low when losing.
2. You're betting high when winning.

Here is another suggestion that is an option off some of the previous systems. I told you a while back, that when I win on a level-three bet and move to 5 coins, I stay at that max bet for only one play. Then, win or lose, I drop back to the level-three bet and make my next bet based on the result of that play.

Not so in this low/high series. Whether you use the 2/5 or the 3/5 series, when you hit max coins, stay there and continue to play max coins until there is no return on a bet. At that point, you would drop back to the low level you were using and stay there until it kicks off a return.

One other thing to mention, and again I give you the option, is when you use this low/high system in video poker, what do you do with a push? Let's say you are playing a Jacks or Better machine and insert 2 coins. A pair of Queens shows and the buzzer sounds, plus the word *winner* flashes on the board. Of course it ain't a winner because all you get back is the 2 coins you played. But the casinos would have you believe you've won—or maybe they can't spell tye or puch. In any event, you didn't win, so stay at the level of bet you were at, when the lye appears!

I like the low/high theory and encourage an aggressive player, who doesn't like climbing steps, to use it. It's not infallible because you could fall into a chopping pattern, but it's better than playing at a machine and flipping a coin to decide how much to bet.

44

System 14: Baby Steps

This is the fourteenth book I've written on gambling and the second on slots. There is also a book on video poker, that my publisher (Kensington Publishing Corporation) will release in a couple of months. Both of those previous books were completed before this one and go deeper into systems, methods, money management and discipline. I'm telling you this because some of the systems (while admittedly altered with different spinoffs), can be found in all three books. Some were worth repeating, hence you'll find them in all the books.

The method I will go over here is called "baby steps" and maybe you'll read about it in the video poker book, but what the heck, it ain't gonna hurt you to see its value (if you think it has any).

The baby steps system is kind of a mix of the up the steps and the pattern. Maybe some people don't like waiting for a win to appear before upping their bet. Others might like to have a preconceived betting series, which the pattern theory embraces. Here are three sets of series for use at 5-coin machines:

1. a. 2-2-2
    b. 3-3-3
    c. 4-4-4
    d. 5-5-5

2.   a.   1-1-1
     b.   2-2-2
     c.   3-3-3
     d.   5-5-5

3.   a.   2-2-2-2-2
     b.   3-3-3-3
     c.   4-4-4
     d.   5-5

Each series could be played out, unless your loss limit and/or naked pulls reared their ugly head.

You can review the above series and change it to fit your style of betting. Personally I like number three. It goes slowly (baby steps), while reducing the amount of the larger bets. Incidentally, even though you don't have to ask, each bet of every series is made with no dependence on the prior bet (either being a winner or loser). You just take the baby steps through the series.

This allows you to slowly escalate your bets. You know I hate constant max bets because there is always the chance of a long line of losses and you could get whacked.

My friend Ken Plane is always complaining that my methods are too conservative. He told me that he sets his series at max level: 5-5-5-5-5-5-5-5-5-5-5 and on and on. The other day I was walking across the bridge in A.C. and Ken Plane was perched on the rail, threatening to jump. I questioned his intentions. He told me he had lost 123 consecutive max plays at one certain machine and he was devastated at being such a jerk! No, he didn't jump— I pushed!

45

System 15: Play and Run

When I observe the different types of players in the casinos, it's odd how so many have different ideas as to what is the best way to play. None of them is wrong, because if you have a way of playing and it works for you, how can you say it's wrong? The moves that work for me, and have been working for years, are all geared to money management and discipline. In the long run (and the short run, by the way), it all comes down to those two parts of the Big Four.

I see a lot of people going from machine to machine, playing a few coins and moving on. The only problem is that there does not seem to be a consistent pattern to how long they play, and most of all, I see a big difference in how many coins or pulls that they apply to each machine.

I am not condemning the method, but I would like to offer my 2 cents as to how to put together a little package to use with this method. I call it the "play and run." It is not to be confused with another of my theories in the casino, called the "hit and run." It is designed for those people who have a small bankroll to operate with and cannot lay out large session amounts. It is for those people with Swiss cheese bankrolls (lotta holes in it), and yet will let them take $50 to battle and take shots at a bevy of machines.

Let's say you have $50 and wanna spread it out over three to four hours:

1. Divide $50 into ten machines at $5 each.

2. Buy-in at a machine for $5 and set naked pulls and loss limits.

3. You have twenty plays at 25 cents each and you remain right at that single-coin play.

4. You do not increase even after a win.

5. The chicken system, if you recall, allows you to pick a betting method, this one does not—you play 1 coin.

6. If after a series of 20 quarters is played and you have *any* loss, you leave the machine.

7. If you had set your naked pulls and reached it before the twenty plays, you're gone.

8. You do *not* play from credits, *absolutely not.* You insert 1 coin at a time.

9. The session is over after twenty plays.

10. If you have *any* profit, rat-hole those coins and start another twenty-play series at the same machine.

11. You can stay at this machine as long as the 1-coin twenty-play series shows a profit, any profit.

12. The last play of *any* series cannot be a *win.* Play until your last insertion is a loss.

13. Repeat: Rat-hole (set aside) every profit over your starting 20 coins, every series.

The outlay is small, the potential profit is small, but you're playing with a small stake. You will last a long time and maybe, just maybe, your travels will take you to a *hot* machine.

46

System 16: Howie's System

I've mentioned this method in other books and you might also find it interesting. There are some excellent reasons for you to want to play it and the back-end possibilities offer several options.

Howie G. is my partner in the company that makes videos, handles seminars, etc., and he resides in Las Vegas. Veterans of sports betting will understand this next message. I bet sports 364 days a year, and so do thousands of others, Howie included. We start working on our picks, as soon as the "line" is released each day.

Several years ago, after an early breakfast and a quick figuring of the early games for a baseball schedule, Howie and I stopped into a local sports parlor, Little Caesar's, to start our work day. The lines were still being finalized and we had several minutes to kill. Little Caesar's featured sports betting and attracted most players with that interest. There were a couple of blackjack and craps tables, empty, and several rows of slots. Howie told me about a system that he used at the machines and told me to get a couple of rolls of quarters and he would show me the play. (I think he charged me for the info, but I won it back at gin rummy.)

We walked around the slot section until we found a machine where the last play was a winning one but the customer took his coins and left that machine. Howie also believes in trends and he rightfully explained that this machine was obviously on a streak, even though we could only see the last play and result. When we got to that machine, Howie put 6 coins aside. "I make three plays of 2 coins each. If nothing happens, I leave that machine, with total investment of $1.50 but if I win a bet with any of those three plays, I go to max-(3-)coin play."

We played at that machine for a couple of minutes, until he lost three in a row. He put several coins in his pocket and we went searching for another machine that was showing a win but was not being played.

I was able to grasp the system in about twenty seconds and said it wasn't fair that I had to pay for it. Howie G. did not relent. (I couldn't wait for the chance to get him at gin rummy.)

I remember walking around Little Caesar's that morning, playing only slots and only where the prior play was a win. I also remember pocketing $26 for about an hour's play. To this day, whenever I see either a video poker or slot machine that is showing a payoff and is empty, I play several coins.

You can adjust the amount of plays:

1. Find a machine that shows a payoff.

2. Make sure it is empty. I don't think a person playing a slot that just hit, would appreciate it if you pushed him aside.

3. Predetermine (and stick to) a series that you intend to play.

4. Leave when three straight losses occur.

Method has merit because it does get you into trends, or if it is cold, an early exit. I got my money that Howie charged me back in gin rummy that afternoon. It's been eight years since he showed me that system. I haven't beaten him in gin rummy since . . .

47

Minimizing Losses

I've already gone over loss limits but maybe some of you were not listening and in case you weren't, I'd like to stick a quick reminder in here, about cutting down losses. You'll notice that practically all of the systems I have outlined in this section have to do with holding losses down. Well, that is, in my humble opinion, the key to winning. There are veteran casino gamblers that ain't gonna read this book because they don't play slots. But they do play table games and they get whacked on occasion. Why do they get whacked? Good question, glad you asked. Because they don't hold down their losses on days when they are losing.

Oh, have I said that before? It must be important. It is just as important in playing the slots as it is for the table game players.

Zero in on the systems and the methods of betting that surround this chapter. They are geared to help you, not hinder your chances of winning.

I bet on sporting events, such as football, basketball, and baseball 364 days a year. I don't win every day but I win more than I lose.

When I am losing, I cut my bets back until the trend changes, and when I hit a winning streak, my bets are escalated. The key message in this paragraph was about betting small when losing. It's called minimizing losses.

I tell you this because I am trying to help you grasp the importance of having the benefit of my advice. Is it good advice?

It is fabulous, my friend, because I know the hurt that comes from losing, and I learned how to control that hurt, by cutting my losses. Is this the last time I will talk about minimizing losses? Nope! But if I can convince just one person, just one, to follow my guidelines, then the chapter was well worth the ink.

Were you the one who got convinced this time?

48

System 17: The Ladder

I don't think I don't got no ego, but anybody who writes books or paints pictures or creates things sometimes falls in love with his projects. Here is a case in point. In my slots book I put in a chapter called "The Ladder." I started writing about the system and glanced at that chapter. It was so good, that I decided to reprint it in full. So if you read the slots book, you already know this method. It's a pretty good system, but what the heck, I say that about all my writings (grin).

The reason I give names to these systems is so that if you pick one of these approaches you'll be able to identify the method and zero in on that play or one of its spinoffs. I number the systems for reference purposes. This way you can remember the approach by either name or number. The number method helps my friend Ken E. Spell, who cannot spell, so he needs numbers.

On the other hand, my lady friend Miss Dee Kount doesn't know a 2 from a 9. She missed the count fourteen consecutive years on New Year's Eve and to this day hasn't got a clue as to what day it is or for that matter what month. She needs me to give these systems names, cause Miss Dee Kount would miss a number reference over and over. So system 17 will be called the ladder. It is a perfectly easy theory to grasp, cause the approach is just like you would be going up a ladder: one step at a time.

In fact it is very close to the basic "up the steps" system, except that the ladder method does not give you the opportunity of staying at a particular level for periods of time. The ladder system always goes up or down by ones and never repeats at any level. You wouldn't wanna stand on any rung of a ladder for long periods, unless you were compelled to do so because of a certain job or chore you were doing at a certain level. But since the basic purpose of the ladder is to go up or down, I use the theory to keep your bets moving up and down. You go "up" the ladder as you win, you go "down" the ladder as you lose.

Your bets are all tied into series and there will be many, many series at each session. Naturally the obligatory naked pulls and loss limits apply and I repeat that "broken record" message to make sure you never forget it!

The series always starts in the middle of the maximum coins required. Since you're at a 5-coin machine, your series starts with 3 coins. This way you have the chance to go up if a win occurs and down if a loss is the result.

Your first bet is 3 coins. If you lose, you play 2. If you win, you go back to 3, lose again, go to 2, lose, go to 1. If you win again go to 2. Again if you lose, you must bet 1. Notice you're reducing your bets after a loss, increasing after a win. When you drop to 1 coin and lose three times in a row, that series is over and you start again with 3 coins. By the same token, a few consecutive winning pulls will get you to 5 coins, which would be the maximum. If you bet the 5 coins and win, bet 5 again; win, bet 5 again—a few losses occur and you're down to 1 again. Three losses at 1, and that series is over.

A new series has begun and you follow the same pattern. The series tend to be quick with the ladder system, but the purpose is a controlled way of playing and trying to get you into the habit of winning small amounts consistently.

If you're at a cold machine, the guidelines of loss limits will hold those losses way down. Just keep a close watch on your session amount and don't exceed the loss limits. This is a snap to grasp.

49

Offshoots of the Ladder

You already know that the 5-coin machine calls for your series to start in the middle, with a 3-coin shot. A win calls for a decrease to the next lowest amount. It's not hard to understand what to bet, my concern is that you grasp the reasons for doing so. In simple logical terms it merely means you bet higher as you win, and bet lower as you lose.

The subsequent bets off of the previous play are only affected by single increases or decreases. In other words, a win at the 3 level means your next bet is 4 coins, not a jump to 5. If you lost at the 3-coin play, your next play is 2 coins. You only move one step at a time.

The drawback to this system is obvious and I addressed it in the previous chapter. It has to do with the fact that the series end very quickly because as soon as you reach the betting unit of 1 coin and lose three consecutive plays, you must go back to the 3-coin level to begin a new series. If you keep winning and reach the 5-coin play, let's say another win occurs, stay at 5 coins as long as you keep winning. A loss drops you to 4 coins.

One tiny drawback: suppose you're in a series and you bet 4 coins and lose. Your next bet must be 3 and again you lose. You bet 2 and lose again! Another blank occurs as you bet 1 coin, which gives you four losses in a row.

You haven't hit your naked pulls or loss limits yet, but when you get to the end bet in the ladder system, your series is over after three straight losses at the first level and calls for the start of a new series. That means you gotta jump to a 3-coin bet, which goes against my basic theory of betting small as you get into a losing streak. But the ladder has its own rules and even though you're in a losing streak of four, five, six, or seven in a row, you jump up to a 3-coin bet. I realize it ain't like I'm telling you to walk on broken glass, eat fire, or give up eating for six hours, but I am telling you to jump your bet after a loss. It hurts me to make this suggestion but that's the nature of the ladder system.

My friend Al Sink has taken a close look at this method and sees both the good and bad. "I'll think about it" says Al Sink, which is all I'm asking every one of you to do. All of these systems are controlled disciplined money-management moves, presided over by win goals and loss limits. They are geared to get you away from cold machines and keep you at hot ones.

But most of them program your every single solitary bet. Therein lies the power of my theory. Your every move is predetermined with no excuse for error. So if Al Sink can take the time to think about which system he thinks is best for him, then I think you oughta think about what Al Sink is thinking about and not sink back to your old haphazard way of playing.

I *sink* it's time to move to the next chapter.

50

System 18: The Umbrella

I want to get across the point that these systems are not geared to make you rich. They are strictly a tool to control every single solitary bet you make. No longer will you just pop coins in without a predetermined method or system to guide you.

Speaking of systems, here's one called "the umbrella," due to the fact that the bets always start small, work up to a long run at maximum coins, and then work back down to smaller ones. Sure, it's "just another pattern" but it does interest both the small bettor and the aggressive player because you can adjust how much you play at each level. Remember that the absolute maximum amount you can bet at any level is 5 coins. Here are some sample series:

- 1-1-3-3-5-5-4-4-4-2-2
- 1-1-1-4-4-5-5-5-3-3-2-2-2
- 1-1-4-4-5-5-5-3-3-2-2
- 1-1-1-1-3-3-3-5-5-5-4-4-4-2-2-2-2
- 1-4-4-5-5-5-3-3-2
- 1-1-3-3-5-5-5-4-4-2-2

Take a look at the patterns for the umbrella system. Surely you've picked up the basic purpose by now. It's in the fact that the bets start small, work up to the max of 5 coins, stay there for a few pulls, and then start back down to the 2-coin pull. Look at those examples again. Notice that you creep up to the 5-coin max and stay there for two or three pulls before you drop down again.

You can also employ patterns whereby you use the same theory of getting to the max and then repeating the same pattern back down to the minimum play. Take a look:

- 1-2-3-4-5-5-5-4-3-2-1
- 1-1-3-3-5-5-3-3-1-1
- 1-1-2-2-3-3-4-5-4-3-3-2-2-1-1
- 1-1-3-3-5-5-5-3-3-1-1
- 1-1-2-4-5-5-4-2-1-1
- 1-1-1-3-4-5-5-5-4-3-1-1-1

Notice that every series starts small and after reaching the max amount comes right down to the first bet with equal-play amounts on either side of the maximum bet.

None of the series stayed at the 5-coin play for long, so I'll give you a couple:

- 1-1-2-3-4-5-5-5-5-5-4-3-2-1-1
- 1-2-2-3-4-4-5-5-5-5-3-2-2-1
- 1-1-3-4-5-5-5-5-4-3-1-1
- 1-1-2-3-4-4-5-5-5-5-4-4-3-2-1-1

This is not a bad approach because it works up to the max bet and stays there for several pulls. The drawback is that you keep going up with your bets, regardless of the results of the previous pull. For instance, look at the second line in the last set of examples. After four pulls you're in the max territory of 5 coins for four straight pulls.

You have your loss limits and naked pulls to protect you, but the fact that you're betting 5 coins after perhaps four or five losses can be expensive. Try this method with a series that starts off with a string of 1-coin bets and goes up slowly. The series could be long, but if it cuts losses, what could be wrong with it? Try something like this:

- 1-1-1-1-2-2-3-5-5-5-3-2-1-1-1-1

You can start with a series like this one, or an even more conservative approach if that is your choice.

After the series ends and you have a profit for that session, revert to the guarantee and excess theory. Rat-hole a profit, which is your guarantee, and proceed at the same machine with the excess. You say you don't understand the guarantee and excess theory? Then get your hide back to that chapter and learn it! Now!

51

System 19: The Shotgun

You know the damage a shotgun can do. It spreads bullets all over the place, hitting not only the broad side of a barn but the outhouses on both sides and the backside of an old bull minding his own business a hundred feet away from the barn.

That's the good part of the shotgun—it spreads the scores all over the place. But it also has a bad side. When it does hit something, the bullets spray so much that very little damage is done. The broad side of the barn has only a few holes in it and even the outhouse doesn't crumble under the spray.

Of course, if you tell that old bull that the buckshot hanging out of his behind really doesn't hurt, you'll get his version of a soft-shoe number, which he'll gladly perform on the part of your anatomy where the sun don't shine. But all in all, the shotgun has some instances where it scores a lot, but not often enough, if you catch my drift.

So the system we'll go over now is called "the shotgun." That's because you're gonna take a shot at a row of machines where you won't do much damage to your bankroll, but you may hit on a number of small machines, maybe six, where you'll put your plan into play.

Actually, you're taking a shot at all six machines, not just one, hoping at least one of them is ripe for a score. You set up your pattern of play, but this system is not aimed at just one machine, rather, it's aimed at how much you'll put into each of the machines. We'll start with the first machine where you deposit 1 coin and pull. Then deposit 2 coins and pull. Then deposit 3 coins and pull, then 4 coins, and last 5 coins. Then you move on to the next machine, except if one of the plays kicks off a score. In that instance, you gotta repeat the amount of coins you played, because you *never* leave a machine where your last play was a winning one. Or have I said that? Yes, I have. I've said it before!

Each machine of the six that you picked out gets the same level of play. All the machines must be the same, i.e., 5-coin machines (you can also play this at the 3-coin slots).

Even my foreign friend from France, Count de Kennot III, who does most of his gambling in Monte Carlo, can't count the number of toes he has on both feet, but he has mastered the art of counting to 5. That's all he needs to make this system work. You pick the six machines, arrive at a session amount, lay out your series, and go right down the line. It's as easy as 1-2-3-4-5.

1. Pick six machines.
2. Set aside 15 coins for each.
3. Set naked pulls and loss limits.
4. Deposit coins in the pattern of 1-2-3-4-5.
5. When the six machines have been played, the series is finished.

Go back and start over.

Even if Count de Kennot III cannot count the number of wives he has, these five steps will be easy for him to remember. The theory of the shotgun is that one, two, or even three of those machines will kick off a return. The most you are investing in a machine is the total of the series 1-2-3-4-5, which equals 15 coins or $3.75 at the quarter slots. Of course, if you wanna play at a higher-stakes machine, you can—providing that your bankroll allows it. You know that I'm gonna suggest playing the lowest stakes machine.

If you have a small stake, simply cut down your series to 1-2-3. That means that at the quarter slots you're risking $1.50 per machine and $9 for the whole group of six machines. You can vary the number of coins you put in, as well as varying the number of machines you play. Again, your bankroll will determine how many machines and how many coins you can play.

The shotgun gives you a couple of shots at several machines. You ain't gonna win a lot of money at one machine, but you ain't gonna do much damage to your bankroll either.

52

Wrapping Up Systems

Well, I think you got a bellyful of systems to use at the machines, whether they be slots or video poker. Several of the approaches were duplicates (like the ladder) of methods I put into my original slots book and original video poker book.

What am I supposed to do? If I bypass those systems and try to con you into believing there are dozens of new plays to try, then I'd be gypping those people who never saw the original writings and would be deprived of these powerful moves.

Yes, they *are* powerful! They cause you—rather *demand* that you use money management when playing the machines. Playing the slots is no different than any other gambling outlet, where you risk your money on the outcome of a decision, or have I said that before?

Will these methods work all the time? Of course not, but the naked pulls and loss limits are put there for that purpose, to get you away from cold machines.

Yesterday (again) I drove to the A.C. casinos and they were packed. Not crowded, but packed, on a cold windy Sunday in the beginning of February. I played a little craps at a cold table and won about $120 before wrapping up the session when two shooters in a row beat me. There were no other tables to get involved with, because of the crowd. So I headed to the slot and video poker section and decided to try my hand at Jacks or Better.

Good luck! There were no empty machines. I killed an hour walking around, observing the hundreds of people pouring max coins after max coins into every play. You could tell by the looks on their faces and their mannerisms that they were floating downstream with no help in sight.

I eventually found a machine, bought in for $40 and played the high/low. A guy sitting next to me was betting max coins on every single pull, three separate times, stopping to insert a $10 new buy-in.

One time I got four 6s with 2 coins in. The guy next to me, while inserting another bill into his machine, remarked, "Hey, you only had two coins in, you should have been playing the max."

I told him my machine was kind of cold and I was waiting for it to heat up. He blew away my explanation. "Hey, the only way you can win is by taking a big shot and betting the max coins." I merely nodded. I don't believe in talking to walls.

About twenty minutes later, after a couple more sawbucks went south, the guy left his machine, grumbling something about his sons and witches, at least it sounded like that. I know he lost his shirt, but then he said playing max was the only way to win.

I left about a half hour later when my machine showed its down side. I cashed in for $87, making me a $47 victor. If I was playing max coins, I'd be coming out *victim* instead of *victor.*

Should you use systems? What do you think?

53

Reality: Yeah, Again

I know, you don't wanna hear this again, but I told you that the reality of gambling is that we have such a fine line to walk between winning and losing that it is imperative that we "learn how to win."

What does that mean, "learn how to win"? Glad you asked, because there are thousands of people who head to the casinos every day, thinking that their winnings will put them in fat city.

That is not the real world. That is not reality, in the life of gambling. That kind of thinking is strictly garnered by the idea that people win millions of dollars every year and you'd like to be a part of that bonanza.

If you'll notice in the casinos, whenever a person does hit a jackpot on the slots, you have to wait a half hour for the slot host to come over and shut down the bells on that machine. They want those bells and whistles to sound off because it gives the other players the idea that they, too, can hit the big one.

Once that host comes over and shuts down the noise and takes the information about how much cash you are to receive, they leave the lights blinking, proclaiming to the world that another player took a big chunk of cash from the casino coffers.

I *know* you wanna bang out a big payday but keep in mind what you are fighting when attacking those machines. Think about how many times you took $200 to the casinos and got ahead $60, $70, or even $100. That's an excellent return for the money you have at risk. Do you quit? Of course not, it's too early, and maybe you'll win more. Sure you will! And I'm gonna find $100,000 on the seat of my car when I get to the parking garage.

Of course you could use the guarantee and excess method that I explained before, whereby you at least take home 50 percent of what you got ahead. But not many of you will do that. I also told you that if you had all facets of the Big Four, your chances of winning was still only 50-50. How many of you listened?

Tomorrow I'll be heading back down to A.C. with my bankroll. I'd love to triple that amount, but between you and me, I'll be ecstatic if I come home with my starting bankroll and a 20-30 percent profit. I'll gladly quit if I get up that much. Because I know the reality of gambling and the power of that chip.

Since we're talking about having the brains and guts to quit with small profits, may I repeat (again) my favorite message? I feel a lot of shaking heads but I'll repeat it anyway. "Seventy percent of the people who enter a casino get ahead . . . yet 90 percent of that 70 percent give the money back!"

Tch, tch, tch—what dorks!

54

Who Has Money Management?

The answer to that question is pretty simple. The people who have money management are the people who really wanna win at gambling. I don't mean people like my friend Ed N. Sand, who has his head in the sand when it comes to grasping the true pitfalls of gambling. He thinks gambling is gonna be the end-all for all of his money problems.

He reads about people hitting the jackpot in the casinos for a half million dollars or someone banging the lottery for three million and he figures it's snap city to turn a fortune himself. Naturally he doesn't factor in the millions of people who play the slots or who take shots on the lottery. He only sees what the casinos and the states want you to see—that someone won.

So Ed N. Sand comes up for air and decides to take his last $300 to the casinos for his chance to become wealthy. On the drive to the casinos, he promises God that he won't cheat on his wife for three months, if God will just let him win the jackpot. Then he catches himself, "Er, God, better make that three days, I don't wanna go overboard with promises!"

Lo and behold, fifteen minutes after playing at the machines, Ed N. Sand bangs out a $3,000 jackpot. Bells are ringing, people staring, and old Ed is figuring out all the bills he can pay with his windfall.

He gets his money and figures, "Hey, if I can win $3,000 in fifteen minutes, imagine what I can do in a couple of hours, with this starting stake." He heads back to the machines but this time he runs into cold trend after cold trend. The more he loses, the higher he bets.

Pretty soon he's down to only a $500 profit and starts praying to God "just let me win back the money I invested." The fates ain't buying that request. Within three hours, the $3,000 jackpot is gone, so is the $300 starting bankroll and so is the money from two trips to the credit-card machines. You know the rest because it has happened to you or someone you know. He loses everything!

How do I know so much about people like Ed N. Sand? Because that was me, years ago. I never took the time to realize how important it was to get ahead and quit.

Why couldn't this jerk just take a few hundred to re-invest and if that failed—go home. He has no money management and if you see yourself in this story—*even on a lesser dollar scale,* then you don't have money management either!

Well, you better get it!

55

Wrapping Up Money Management

You've heard of ham and eggs, Abbott and Costello, Martin and Lewis, Ozzie and Harriet, Tom and Jerry, fire and brimstone, up and down, and over and under. Seems like if we mention one, the other comes to mind. In many cases they more or less help each other out and even in some cases, one could not exist without the other. Well, what has that got to do with gambling in general and slots in particular? Glad you asked, so I'll mention two subjects and see if you can see the connection: money management and discipline.

See the connection? One is pretty much related to the other and quite honestly, both actually depend on each other to reach a happy result. We're aware that both are part of the Big Four in gambling, so right away we know they are important to our gambling days.

I've already told you that money management is: "Knowing what to bet after a win and what to bet after a loss." It is the controlling of money you have on hand, to protect it from being wasted during losing streaks and to make sure it is properly handled during winning streaks and hot trends. The words and the message pretty much sums it up: money management is managing your money.

Even my friend Ina Fogg, who loses all sight of reality in a casino and walks around in a fog, can grasp what money management is all about.

That is why I gave you several methods of betting, called systems. They are designed to show you how to "manage your money" with every bet you make at a machine. That is money management. But right next to that requirement is a thing called discipline. This "blessing" gets its own section coming up, but it is important that you see the correlation between money management and discipline.

One works on and feeds off the other. One is useless without the other. You can use the money management moves to improve your bankroll, but if you don't use the discipline to quit and take advantage of the positive position that the money management methods put you into—then both categories will destroy each other.

It's like building a house. You wouldn't build a house and not put a roof over it, to cap your accomplishment. Then you shouldn't get ahead in gambling and not cap it off with the discipline factor. Are you ready for discipline? Maybe you won't like the rules regulating discipline. But you sure as heck will like the results!

PART V

Discipline

56

Discipline

Ah, discipline! The fourth and final part of the Big Four. The part that is by far the hardest to put into your game plan. You hear people say all the time:

1. I have discipline in everything I do.
2. My children are very disciplined.
3. Kids need discipline, both at home and in school.
4. He is a very disciplined person.
5. I've been a coach for twenty years and my players always have discipline.
6. I teach tap dancing and stress discipline to all my students.
7. It takes discipline to do anything in life.

We hear all those statements from time to time and the last one (number 7), pretty much sums it all up.

We all need discipline and it is the disciplined (prepared) person who is usually the most successful. Go back over those seven so-called statements and see if you haven't said them or heard them several times.

You probably agree with most of them because discipline is so important in everything we do. Then why in heaven's name, do people who believe in discipline enter a casino and break every single disciplined idea that ever entered their minds?

May I repeat for my friend Rhee Repeat, who needs things repeated many times before she grasps the message. You've heard it before, so you can skip the next sentence (but you won't because you know dang well that it is aimed at you): "Seventy percent of the people who enter a casino get ahead, at some time during the course of their day, yet 90 percent of that 70 percent give the money back."

What dorks they are, what illogical reasoning to not know enough to quit with a profit.

Question: Why do they break the rules of discipline? Good question, glad you asked.

Answer: Because they are dorks and have no discipline!

If the shoe fits—wear it!

57

Why Is Discipline Important?

Why is putting your socks on first, before putting your shoes on important? Because it is the logical thing to do. If you can invent a way to get your socks on, after your shoes are in place, you'll be a very rich person. In a like manner, trying to win money without having the discipline to set up a win goal ahead of time, will have you constantly falling short of a successful day.

The message I repeated to you in the last chapter admits that people can get ahead. That really is not a problem for many people. But once you get to that situation, unless you have the prior intelligence to have set a win goal, then you never know when to quit, when to pack it in.

Setting that win goal ahead of time, just like setting a loss limit, is done so as to protect your money, both on days when you get ahead and on days when nothing is going well. Enter discipline, probably the most important part of capping off the Big Four. It ain't easy, but it is important.

In Atlantic City, the casinos have deals with travel agencies and bus companies throughout New Jersey, New York, Pennsylvania, Connecticut and other close-by states. They pay the freight for getting these customers to their casinos by giving the patrons a cash coupon, lunch, gifts, etc., just to get them to those row upon row of machines. One of the stipulations is that you have to stay six hours before the bus heads back to your original destination. Six hours!

A lot of these people have $300, $200, even $100 to gamble. Spread over six hours, minus an hour for lunch, that leaves a lot of time to attack those chip-infested slot machines. Why do they want you to stay six hours, or even four hours? Don't tell me you ain't figured it out yet!

Because the casino bigwigs *know* that the longer you walk the aisles between those one-armed bandits, you'll dip into your money, whether ahead or behind. They *know*, you don't have the discipline to abstain from playing, waiting for that danged bus.

Why is discipline important? Because most people lack it in the casinos and the breaking of those disciplined rules that you follow in the real world go down the drain when surrounded by the buzz of excitement and bright lights of casino land.

So, if you got the discipline to put your socks on before your shoes, because it's the logical thing to do, then you should set up disciplined stops in the casino—because it's also the logical thing to do.

58

Who Has Discipline?

I don't need ten fingers and ten toes for this answer. About a half dozen gambling types have this intelligence factor at their beck and call. Who has discipline?

1. Professional gamblers.
2. People who know how tough it is to win at gambling.
3. People who set intelligent win goals (20 percent to 30 percent).
4. People who previously lost constantly in gambling and finally learned to enjoy even small returns.
5. People who realize that on losing days, setting a loss limit (50 percent) is also a form of discipline.
6. People who predetermine their aforementioned win goals and loss limits.

Maybe I left off a couple of people, but you get the idea. See if you can find yourself in any of those six categories. If you're in all of them, you don't need any advice from me. The funny thing is that many people who are disciplined in their normal routines, leave the Big D at the door, when they enter a casino.

My friend Dee C. Plinn claims she has a lot of discipline in her life and she does. When going to the supermarket, she will bring $96.39 and a hand-held adding machine to keep track of her purchases. Each time she puts an item in the basket, she records the price on her adding machine. She doesn't spend one penny over the predetermined amount she brings to spend. Last week it took her fifteen minutes to sort through eleven different brands of sauerkraut, till she finally found one where she saved 3 cents per can and 14 cents if she bought a case. Naturally she bought the case of sauerkraut. How can you turn down a nice savings of 14 cents? It only took her four and a half hours to do her shopping, but when she got home, her discipline saved her $1.22, for which she was ecstatic.

The next day she went to Atlantic City and blew $650 on her credit card, playing the dollar slots, in an attempt to "hit the big one," and at the same time have a nice day out. I asked Dee C. Plinn where her discipline was and she was shocked at my question! "Hey, I have more discipline than anyone. I bring an amount of money I can afford to lose, and when it's gone, so am I." And off she stalked.

That's discipline? I call it stupidity. It is a total lack of the grasp of what discipline is all about.

Who has discipline? Go back and read the half dozen examples in the front of this chapter. If you don't find yourself in one of those categories—you're in a lot of trouble!

59

"Afford to Lose"

I ain't gonna spend a lot of time in this chapter explaining the stupid title above. Maybe you've already figured out where I'm going on this one. It is part of the answer I get, time after time, in seminars when I pose the question, "How much money do you bring to the casinos?" Invariably, as if on cue, someone states, "Oh, I bring an amount of money I can afford to lose!"

The nodding of heads by many other people in the room clue me in that I am among the clueless (the main part of the title of this book). I ask for a show of hands by those who agree with the explanation of the original stater. Sure enough, about 50 percent of the attendees show their approval by reaching for the sky.

I walk over to the originator of this statement and ask a couple of questions:

1. Are you independently rich?
   Answer: No!

2. Do you have a lot of money to throw around?
   Answer: No!

3. Do you really have an extra $300 or $400 to blow in a casino?
   Answer: Not *really.*

4. Can you sit there and honestly tell me you can *afford* to lose
    $300 or $400 in one day on gambling?

Answer: I guess not!

Then I repeat the stupid statement, "Money I can *afford* to lose!"
And let the message sink in. What a stupid analogy to even let
enter the vast caverns of your head, as it pertains to gambling.

Some will reply that, "Hey, it's entertaining and is the same as
going to dinner and a show, and usually costs that much!" My reply
to them is, "OK, you go to dinner and a show and have a few
drinks afterward to cap off a nice night with your wife. On the way
home you feel good that you both enjoyed the evening.

"Now take a day at the casinos where you and your wife
dropped $200 at the slots. On the way home, you barely speak to
each other, except to ask if you want fries with your hamburger,
while grabbing a bite at the nearest burger stop."

How come it doesn't count as entertainment for that blown
$200? No, you don't bring money you can afford to lose—it's just
a stupid statement made by people who wanna give an excuse for
their losses.

Think about that title for a second: *"Afford to lose money."*

No wonder they build stalls for donkeys!

60

License to Steal

You've heard the term and know what it means. For those of you, like my friend Don Noe, who don't know what it means, but repeat the statement themselves, it is a sarcastic inference against people and places that they think are (for want of a better word) screwing them.

People who lose in the casinos can often be heard uttering these words as they examine their empty wallets and pocketbooks and head for their cars for the agonizing ride home. They are obviously blaming the casinos for their rotten run of fortune on a given day. Hey, if you can't blame the casinos, who can you blame?

Try looking in the mirror! No, that would be too logical. That would be like admitting that *you* did something wrong, and heaven forbid we do something like that.

Years ago I made the same silly stupid remarks. I'd blame everything and everybody for my losses. There were days when I would be ahead a couple of thousand dollars, yet gave it all back—on the same day!

Those were the times Vegas was, well Vegas. I mean the real gambling mecca of the world. There weren't many casinos, the shows were all free, and lounge performers were on stage all day long for your enjoyment. The table minimum was as low as $1, $2, and $3. Roulette tables had 10-cent coins ready for anyone who wished to indulge.

I know, I dealt at several of those tables when I was broke (and that was quite often). People would come up to the table with twenty bucks and play for hours on a few rolls of dimes. Slot machines were precomputer chip, and randomness allowed for jackpots ringing out constantly. The town cried out for players. Meals were $2.95, rooms were $19 with the lushest accommodations, and living was a step below heaven.

But I still kept losing because I was a dork! I didn't know how to win, or rather how to quit a winner. So I blamed the casinos and said, "Man, they got a license to steal."

Well, the years passed, people discovered Las Vegas and turned it into a commercial haven. The price of meals jumped, as did the cost of rooms. The table minimums skyrocketed and the computer geniuses gave us the slot and video poker chip, which makes sure the machines stay within the allotted payoff requirements.

But the casinos don't cheat. They don't have a license to steal. They don't have to. All they gotta do is get you into their casinos and you become "your own worst enemy." Because you don't have the brains (discipline) to *learn how to win!*

61

A Sad Story

I want you to read this chapter. I want you to concentrate on the details, so that maybe you'll see yourself, or someone you know, that fits the pattern. Maybe it will help you avoid this happening to either yourself or someone you know. It is a common happening but because this one happened so recently, and since I was writing about discipline, it figures to be worth inserting here.

In three hours I will be making the two and a half hour trip to the casinos. It's a long ride down and a long ride back. But I'll have company. I take my mother to A.C. twice a week and she loves it. She'll play video poker and slots and maybe, if the tables are not crowded, a little Pai Gow poker or Let It Ride. But most of all, she packs a lunch of goodies that I can devour on the trip. I wonder if that's the only reason I bring her—well, that's another story.

Anyhow, yesterday I received a call from a lady named Jean, from Minnesota. She wanted to discuss gambling with me and wanted suggestions on which games to play. This is not uncommon because I get about 200 phone calls, letters, messages, and emails every week. The same questions are asked. I give the same answers.

As we spoke, little by little, she told me things about herself, as I have the "knack" of getting personal, without seeming to get personal, if you know what I mean.

It turns out she has read my slots book (the original one, with over thirty systems in it). She has it memorized and also agrees with the loss limits, win goals, naked pulls, guarantee and excess, etc. Then she gets to the casino and the aura (her words) takes over. She can't stop playing. She can't quit, whether winning or losing.

Jean is seventy-one years old, living with her retired husband and they have (had) a nice nest egg put aside to enjoy when retirement came. Jean was involved in an accident several years ago and received a couple of settlement checks, which were quickly deposited to their account. They ain't there now. It seems her and her husband (and then she alone) visited the Indian casinos that are close by. In the beginning everything was so neat and simple. She would win a couple of dollars and quit. Not so one day.

On that day she lost $400. She knew she'd win it back, but lost $550 in the chase. She kept going back, vowing to recoup the losses and graduated to the dollar slots. The losing continued and two weeks ago, $4,000 more went down the drain. She was devastated. She told me this actually happened at one of the dollar machines. There were 117 consecutive pulls with *no return.*

That I questioned but she swore to me it was true. I asked her about naked pulls, trends, and cold machines. She said she felt the machine was *due,* and if she walked away, someone else would reap the rewards.

We talked for over an hour. Her savings are terribly diminished. Her husband does *not* know of this. Her husband does not *know* of this. Yeah, I repeated that sentence. She wanted to know what she should do, and what games she should play to recoup. This story is true. I don't know if you can feel for this lady, but I sure can. She is in big trouble and this terrible plunge by her will affect her family. Because of my constant asking, she finally admitted that four to five times, in the middle of her bad run, she would be ahead $100 or $200 but couldn't stop because she was so far behind overall.

Does all this sound familiar? If it doesn't, then rest assured, it is not an isolated case. Maybe losing $8,000 overall is not big to some of you people, but to Jean, it was a tragedy. I'll talk to her again. But I'll talk to you now. Don't think this, or something like it, can't happen to you—because it can!

62

Chasing the Dream

Did you read the previous chapter? Did you really grasp what Jean is going through? Do you wonder why?

It is "chasing the dream." Hey, we're all privy to dreaming of winning loads of money, to change our style of living, to pay off all those nagging bills, to provide a stable and secure future for our families. And we think gambling will provide us the opportunity to do just that. The combination of gambling and big money is always perceived as running hand in hand.

I talk to people every day who admit that they go to the casinos to win the amount of money that will change their lives. It all seems so easy.

These people ain't crazy, they aren't wrong in their desire to go for a change in their life and lifestyle. The problem is that they don't know how to reach the level of success they dream about.

You've probably bet on the lottery. Just about every state has jumped on the bandwagon, to promote their own state's lottery and even take out ads, telling you to rush to the nearest store to buy your tickets.

People cross state lines to purchase tickets when the amount of winnings climb into the multimillions. These people are chasing their dream. And they ain't wrong for dreaming—only wrong in their approach.

Years ago, the billboards on the highways would always have that nice message scrawled across it: "Have You Hugged Your Child Today?" It made you wanna go right back home and put that suggestion to good use.

Today these same billboards give us a little different message: "Have You Played the Lottery Today?" Imagine that! This message is paid for by the same state agency that takes our taxes and uses part of them to tell us to "gamble" on something that is weighed *drastically* against us.

Then when a winner surfaces, they make sure his name, picture, and background are shown on the front page of all the newspapers, so as to get others to *gamble* on the lottery also.

All this is from a country and group of states that frown on gambling and spend millions each year, cracking down on illegal gambling and bookies. Yet they run their own self-serving lottery! Only in America!

Nah, you ain't wrong in dreaming your dream, or in chasing your dream, but if you go after it in the world of gambling in general and slots in particular, tis time to step back and examine your direction.

The first thing you do is memorize the Big Four. Then you have a spelling quiz. Rearrange the following words:

1. OYMNE AAEETMNMGN
2. NSIICLIDEP

63

Walking

The people who own shoe stores should love me for this chapter. If everyone followed my advice, there would be a huge jump in the sale of shoes, because everyone would be wearing out their stock of footwear.

Telling people to "walk away" from cold machines is like telling a guy who hasn't had a date in three years, to hang up the phone when Miss Universe calls. There is no way either of these things will happen. Just zero in on the prospects of the player who stays at a machine even though it is obvious that the dang thing is cold as ice. I asked my friend Noe Klue, why she stayed at a machine that hadn't kicked off a profit in over an hour. Noe Klue has no clue about discipline, and she proved it by rattling off a few reasons why she stays mired in these poor decisions, to pour good money after lost coins:

1. The machine is due to hit.
2. I told my husband to meet me back here in an hour and I've only been here forty-five minutes.
3. It's only money.
4. I'm comfortable in this seat.
5. All machines are the same.
6. I'll just get rid of this last $10 and then I'll leave.

7. My feet hurt and I don't feel like walking.

8. I ordered a drink and I'm waiting for the waitress.

9. I hit on this machine last year and so losing money back won't hurt me.

If you see yourself in any of these examples, you have a discipline problem. Wait! Let me clarify that last sentence. If you see yourself in any of those examples, you have a problem, *period!*

Yet I have heard each and every one of those excuses for staying at a cold machine, many times over and from many different people. They truly are too lazy to employ the art of walking away from a bad situation, or too dumb to realize that another machine couldn't possibly be as bad as the one they are at.

Walking away from a bad situation in the real world has saved many problems in our everyday lives. Walking away from a bad situation in the casinos is also gonna save you from financial harm. Walk!

1. *W:*   Will insure that you don't get wiped out at a machine.

2. *A:*   And there is always another machine waiting to be hit.

3. *L:*   Loss limits are the key to any type of gambling.

4. *K:*   Kan walking from a cold machine really hurt you?

Kan I help it if I kan't spell? But I sure as heck kan teach you discipline. And it starts with learning how to *walk!*

64

Thinking About Discipline

This is my fourteenth book and I doubt I'll write fourteen more. It all began in 1984 when I wrote my first book on blackjack and continued at about one book a year, up to this point. Way back then, I introduced the Big Four of gambling to an uneducated band of gamblers, who thought (thinks) gambling is simply taking a wad of money to the tables and machines and letting Lady Luck determine the outcome.

Well, that's a bunch of garbage! Luck has nothing at all to do with gambling. It still comes down to the Big Four:

1. Bankroll
2. Knowledge of the game
3. Money management
4. Discipline

With all four of these items, you've got a 50-50 chance of winning. If you are lacking any one of the four, you have a good chance of losing 75 percent to 85 percent of the times you gamble. The suggestions laid out for you on these pages are geared to get you ahead with small profits. The guts to quit is up to each individual.

The two keys to winning constantly are still the same as I outlined in the beginning of the book.

1. Accept small wins
2. Set loss limits

Those two suggestions (demands) are not just for table-game play-ers and sports bettors. They are also pointed at the slot and video poker machine players. Will you listen to the fabulous advice given to you for these past five sections? I don't think so! I think it's too hard for most people to adhere to what it really takes to be a suc-cessful gambler.

My friend Don Sink also don't think he can abide by most of my views. As the clueless Don Sink says, "I don't think you realize what most people think about gambling. They think it is the key to riches. And I think the same way!"

I sink that's enough of that. Give some thought to what I am trying to convey to you. But the pity of it is—that most of you won't!

65

Do's and Don'ts (Etiquette)

This chapter has nothing to do with learning how to win in the casinos, whether at the slots, the video poker machines, or at the table games. It has to do with how you conduct yourself in the casinos, how you handle yourself, respecting contact with other players.

My friend (ex-friend), Ed O. Kett has no etiquette at all. He is a jerk. His careless noncaring actions, while maybe not intentional, bring displeasure to many patrons. Follow him around some day, as he moves around the casino and you'll see why the term "ex" is put in my relationship with him.

Ed O. Kett is a smoker and doesn't care when, why, or where he lights up. Usually it is at a video poker machine where the people on each side of him are subjected to waves of annoying smoke billowing in their direction. He could care less.

I see women more guilty of this act than men, but both groups arouse my anger. When they are done poisoning the lungs of their neighbors and are unable to find an ash tray, they deposit their weapon into the tray where coins are deposited!

Did you ever play at a machine where one of these jerks has dumped his ashes? Check your hands—you're at one.

1. *Don't* smoke where others are *this* close to you!

How about the hog who sits at a slot machine, has his leg draped over one machine to his right, and is leaning back playing the machine to his left. He has effectively wrapped up three machines at a time. This gomb usually waits until a busy Saturday to keep others from playing.

2. *Do* play only one machine at a time.

How about this move, that is generally preferred by video poker players, usually in a casino where there is a scarcity of certain type machines. I'll use Double Joker machines in A.C. as an example. There are only a few available on the floor and usually set in rows next to each other. Ed O. Kett will sit at one machine, *not* playing mind you, but watching his wife at the next machine play her hand. People looking for one of these Double Jokers will ask if he is playing and he'll shoo them away and continue to prevent another player from having this empty machine.

3. *Don't* sit at a machine, especially one that is rare, and not play at it. *Stand* and watch your wife.

Then we have the crybaby. She moans, whines and complains about every single pull of the handle. She tells her sad tale of woe to the poor lady playing next to her, who is experiencing the same frustration.

"Look at that. This is the fourteenth consecutive pull where I got two 7's and nothing on the third reel. These machines are fixed, I ain't coming here again."

4. *Do* stop your whining. You're fighting a chip, so play and shut up, or don't play and shut up, but above all—*shut up!*

At the table games, Ed O. Kett also smokes and tells everyone how to play their hand. He also drinks to excess and at that point becomes an expert in every phase of gambling. He even instructs the dealers how to perform their jobs. Of course he manages to spill his drink on the poor soul sitting next to him, as he reaches to shake hands with the pretty player on the other side of the table.

When the cocktail waitress brings his drink, Ed O. Kett just happens to busy himself with his cards or dice, or checking his watch, or playing with his chips, any number of things to avoid giving her a tip.

5. *Don't* try to be Mr. Personality at a table, where the fact of the matter is that you are lacking in that department—*big time!*

Ed O. Kett has no etiquette. The other players see that. The casino personnel also recognize his shortcomings, but give him plenty of leeway. They know he'll eventually bury himself. Ed O. Kett, the jerk, he brings his own shovel!

66

Wrapping Up Discipline

Well, I guess we've come to the last chapter in the last part of the Big Four. If you ain't gotten nothing out of my words by now, then you're not gonna get it, even if I write seventeen more chapters.

Do you think it's gonna be easy to quit with small profits on a given day, especially when your mind is full of dreams of getting rich on one pull of that one-armed bandit? No, it's not gonna be easy. It's frustrating to be just one click away from realizing your dream of hitting that jackpot and then "settling" for a payday of $60 or $80.

But that's the reality of gambling. It takes a very disciplined person to accomplish success at something, where the odds are stacked against them. Winning in a casino is just such a chore.

My friend Ed N. Sand had his head in the sand when I first gave you the following statement. He wants me to repeat it now for people like Rhee Repeet and I. M. Madork because he feels they are ready to accept the conservative style of betting that I suggest: "Seventy percent of the people who enter a casino get ahead, yet 90 percent of that 70 percent give the money back."

Regardless of what you gamble at, table games, sports, poker, horse racing, or the slots—the key is money management and discipline. And if you can't accept the small percentages that the pros do, at least put yourself in a position of bringing home something! Memorize that statement I repeated above and then leaf back through the money management section and find the chapters that refer to guarantee and excess. This way you'll at least bring home something when you get ahead, and the *excess* move will allow you to then chase your dream of untold riches.

That's *discipline*, which is what you need (better have) if you wanna succeed in gambling.

67

The Ultimate Goal

I know what my ultimate goal is every time I enter a casino: to leave with more money than I started with. I don't give a rat's tail what the profit is. It's the losses that I fear the most. It's a long ride home when your wallet is lighter.

It was easy to rid myself of those frustrating trips by the simple method of *accepting small wins*. By setting my goals at a realistic figure, you'd be surprised how joyful that trip has now become.

As I mentioned several chapters back, this is my fourteenth book. The others are listed here, so that if you ever decide to move to another game, there is a "work of art" just waiting for you to devour its words of wisdom (grin).

1. *Blackjack*
2. *Advanced Blackjack* (card counting)
3. *Craps for the Clueless*
4. *Craps*
5. *Advanced Craps****
6. *Slots*
7. *Baccarat*
8. *Roulette* (advanced)
9. *Roulette/Slots* (discontinued)

Those highlighted by three stars are my favorites. Don't die without reading them. I hope you liked the theories and will heed the messages. If you need to contact me with any questions, please feel free to do so.

Web Page: www.johnpatrick.com
E-mail: johnlpatrick@worldnet.att.net
Phone: 973-992-3862